Welcome to the Funny Farm

The All-True Misadventures of a Woman on the Edge

KAREN SCALF LINAMEN

Fleming H. Revell

A Division of Baker Book House Co
Grand Rapids, Michigan 49516

© 2001 by Karen Scalf Linamen

Published by Fleming H. Revell
a division of Baker Book House Company
P.O. Box 6287, Grand Rapids, MI 49516-6287

Fifth printing, February 2003

Printed in the United States of America

Library of Congress Cataloging-in-Publication Data

Linamen, Karen Scalf, 1960–
    Welcome to the funny farm : the all-true misadventures of a woman on the edge / Karen Scalf Linamen.
        p.   cm.
    ISBN 0-8007-5773-4
    1. Women—United States—Life skills guides. 2. Mothers—United States—Life skills guides. 3. Women—United States—Life skills guides—Anecdotes. I. Title.

HQ1221 .L67 2001
305.4′092—dc21   2001031740

Unless otherwise indicated, Scripture is taken from the HOLY BIBLE, NEW INTERNATIONAL VERSION®. NIV®. Copyright © 1973, 1978, 1984 by International Bible Society. Used by permission of Zondervan Publishing House. All rights reserved.

Scripture marked NASB is taken from the NEW AMERICAN STANDARD BIBLE®. Copyright © The Lockman Foundation 1960, 1962, 1963, 1968, 1971, 1972, 1973, 1975, 1977, 1995. Used by permission.

Scripture marked KJV is taken from the King James Version of the Bible.

Chapter 26 is adapted from myth #7 in *Happily Ever After* (Grand Rapids: Fleming H. Revell, 1997), 86–96. Used by permission.

For current information about all releases from Baker Book House, visit our web site:
http://www.bakerbooks.com

Other books by Karen Linamen

Sometimes I Wake Up Grumpy . . . and Sometimes I Let Him Sleep

Just Hand Over the Chocolate and No One Will Get Hurt

Pillow Talk: The Intimate Marriage from A to Z

Parent Warrior: Protecting Your Children through Prayer

Happily Ever After: And 21 Other Myths about Family Life

I'm Not Suffering from Insanity . . . I'm Enjoying Every Minute of It!

contents

Spring

Summer

Introduction
Welcome to the Funny Farm

About eighteen months ago, I met up with Chris Buri at New Life Clinic, founders of Women of Faith. He told me the organization was launching a web site and asked if I would be interested in writing a weekly humor column.

Thus began "The Funny Farm."

This book contains many of the columns that originally appeared at women-of-faith.com. It also contains some new ones.

More than anything, it contains stories of wild and wacky moments from my life, many of which will be strangely familiar to you because they are probably very much like the wild and wacky moments that occur in YOUR life (if this is indeed true, then you have my condolences).

You'll find stories about the dehydrated gecko my kids make me keep in a jar on top of the refrigerator. Stories about defrosting turkeys with blow-dryers. Stories about AWOL pet tarantulas, wayward waistlines, and how to get sympathy from your dog when there's no one else around to listen to you whine.

You'll also find, sprinkled throughout these tales like the chocolate chips in Toll House cookies, some truths about life, and if you don't think there's a truth about life lurking somewhere in a story about a dehydrated gecko, then read on, dear friend, because you're about to make a discovery.

And the discovery is this: God cares about every aspect of our crazy lives.

Some folks think there's a difference between the secular and the sacred. But the truth is that God is so big that nothing that happens in our lives is outside the circle of who he is or beyond the realm of his great love for us.

It's ALL sacred. Which may seem like an odd way to begin a book that includes the phrase "tandem burping," but when you think about it, it makes a lot of sense.

So when you feel like your life is going crazy . . .

. . . when you need a good laugh to keep from bawling . . .

. . . when you suspect you've got one foot in the Funny Farm and the other foot on a banana peel . . .

. . . take heart. I'm there. I'm with you. In the words of one infamous former president, "I feel your pain."

And here's the best part. God's there. He's there when you find your dog standing on the dining room table sampling the Thanksgiving turkey or when your best friend moves away or when you discover your second chin.

He's there when your kids surprise you with breakfast in bed and you open your mouth for that first bite and glance down at the festive red sprinkles adorning your deviled egg and realize that the aroma filling your nostrils is the scent of cinnamon.

In short, whenever you laugh or cry or sigh or wonder why, God's there, and he's got something good for you: some nugget of insight, chunk of grace, gem of wisdom, or even a chocolate chip of comfort.

So, welcome to the Funny Farm. I hope you have as much fun reading these columns as I had writing them, and may you tap into some inner joy and encouraging insights in the process.

Oh, by the way, next time you feel like you're going crazy, you should give me a call.

I know the way by heart.

Winter

1

No Woman Is an Island

THERE'S A CERTAIN CAMARADERIE AMONG WOMEN.
Whether we're talking about the attitudes of our kids, the contents of our refrigerators, or the girth of our waistlines, we members of the sisterhood of women just seem to have a lot in common.

Maybe it's because we battle so many of the same problems.

Last week I was visiting my folks in Colorado. My mom and I were puttering around together in the kitchen when she said, "Wanna know the best piece of advice I ever got from you?"

Now, I don't normally go around giving advice to my mom— she's a lot wiser than I am—so I was interested to hear what she was about to say. Maybe she had been impressed with some profound insight she'd picked up from something I'd written or while she and I were having an intimate conversation on some deeply spiritual topic.

She said, "It was when you told me to soak crusty pans overnight in automatic dishwashing soap. I haven't scrubbed a pot since."

It's true. If you have a pot or pan with baked-on goo from supper, just fill it with water and toss in some Cascade. The pan wipes clean in the morning.

See? That's what I'm talking about. We all face so many of the same challenges. Whether we're single gals or empty nesters, newlyweds or midlife moms, we all know what it's like to try to scrape the remains of last night's lasagna off our favorite Corningware.

I love it when another woman shares some little tidbit from her own life—an experience or insight—and it's something I've experienced or thought, but figured I was the only one.

I loved it, for example, when a reader wrote to me and confessed that she sometimes cleans her house and then realizes that lurking in the back of her mind is the motivating thought, barely acknowledged, that once her house is clean someone—she doesn't really know who—will arrive at her home and rescue her from all of her troubles. And my eyes blinked wide as I read, and I laughed out loud in amazement.

I thought I was the only one who had experienced that sensation.

I love it when I go to my friend Beth's house. We've been friends for four years now. Not just friends. Close friends. Bosom buddies. And in all our many hours together, I've never once visited her home and used the bathroom frequented by her kids and found the roll of toilet paper ON THE DISPENSER. Not a single time. And I love it because I can relate. In my bathrooms, entire generations of toilet paper rolls will come and go without ever having been introduced to the dispenser next to the toilet. It's as if the dispenser has been relegated to the role of some antiquated appliance that once served a purpose, but has fallen into disuse, like the twenty-pound waffle makers we all used to own or the toaster oven or the rotary dial phone.

But somehow knowing that the dispenser has fallen into disuse at Beth's house too makes me feel a little better. Less guilty. I may still get the Bad Mother of the Year Award for letting my kids manually unwind their toilet paper, but at least I won't be making my acceptance speech all alone. Beth'll be right beside me, sharing the podium. I think one of the scariest feelings in the world is wondering if you're all alone. Of course, I realize that mothers of preschoolers may take issue with this statement because the thing they crave even more than chocolate is isolation. This is because these women have not experienced a private moment—not even to go to the bathroom—since the birth of their first child. But I'm not talking about THAT kind of alone. I'm talking about the alone we feel when we're afraid everyone else is living Martha Stewart/Ruth Graham lives while *our* lives resemble something more akin to Lucy Ricardo meets Roseanne Conner. At Peyton Place, no less.

But that's the nice thing about having friends with whom to share the intimate details of our lives. It helps us realize that we're ALL living Lucy/Roseanne/Peyton Place lives.

King Solomon had it figured out. He wasn't even a woman and he had it figured out (of course, he WAS married to seven hundred of them, so maybe that helped him get a clue). I say he had it figured out because he's credited with writing, in the Book of Ecclesiastes, the observation that "there is nothing new under the sun."

And there isn't.

So the next time you're feeling like no one could possibly understand the things you're going through, think again.

I don't know about you, but I think this is comforting, not because "misery loves company," but because "there's strength in numbers."

And not just strength. There's hope, too. Because if other women have experienced the same struggles and emerged victorious to tell the story, then you and I can do it, too. Although I have to admit, I'm more than a little curious how Solomon's wives made do with baked-on lasagna.

2

No Batteries Required

MY COMPUTER IS WHEEZING.

Would someone please explain this to me?

I realize this is allergy season in some parts of the country, like Texas, where winter doesn't arrive until January and then lasts about as long as an episode of Barney (which, believe me, can FEEL like an eternity, but in reality only lasts for four hours, three if you don't count the commercials).

But I still don't think that explains the rhythmic wheeze coming from my hard drive.

Then again, what do I know? I am technologically impaired. I not only cannot program the VCR, but I'm still figuring out the remote, and I've just recently gotten the hang of programming the microwave.

There should be government aid programs for people like me because, clearly, we are seriously disadvantaged in a culture as hooked on technology as ours is.

Remember when the only digits we had to memorize were the ones in our addresses and phone numbers? To simplify matters even more, phone numbers had a mere five digits because they all started with a word. Mine growing up was Topaz 86957.

Now, the numbers I'm forced to memorize include my home number, fax number, cell phone number, the pin number to my ATM, the access code to my e-mail, the password for my cell phone voice mail, the phone number and passcode to retrieve my answering machine messages . . .

And that's just to keep in touch with *myself*. If I want to actually communicate with another human being, there's an even longer list of home, work, fax, cell phone, and beeper numbers I've got to keep track of.

Maybe my brain's on technology overload. Yeah, that's it. My brain is on overload and, as a result, I have developed a subconscious hostility toward anything that requires a modem, electrical outlet, or battery pack. This would certainly explain why I have such a scary history with things like laptops and cell phones.

Oh. You hadn't heard about the laptop?

Let me begin by saying that any time a woman tells you that she backed over her husband's brand-new laptop computer with her car, you can rest assured there is a perfectly reasonable explanation somewhere.

I'll let you know when I find one.

Until then, let me just say that my husband was going on a trip, and we were loading his bags into the trunk, and the phone rang, and I ran back into the house, and by the time I jumped back in the car and revved the engine it had sort of slipped my mind that the laptop was still sitting on the driveway behind the left rear tire, and, well . . .

I'll let you imagine the rest of the story. Actually, you'll *have* to use your imagination because this is a family-friendly column, and I've been asked to keep the profanity and bloodshed at a minimum.

I'm *kidding.* Actually my husband was amazingly gracious. Which is precisely why, three weeks later when I ran over my cell phone with the van, I felt perfectly comfortable e-mailing him the news and then leaving town for a week. If I'd thought he was going to overreact, I would have stayed away much longer.

Our world is so different than it was just a decade or two ago. Between cell phones, faxes, Federal Express, beepers, laptops, e-mail, e-commerce, and the World Wide Web, the way we talk and shop and think and do business is hardwired to the fast lane.

Which actually is okay. In fact, on a good day—meaning a day when I'm not explaining to a Sprint customer service person why the display on my cell phone looks like a lava lamp—I'll be the first to admit that all this technology can be pretty cool.

Still, I'm glad that some things stay the same. Intimate and old-fashioned, even.

Like talking to Jesus.

What a relief! I don't have to plug in, log on, or boot up. I don't need passwords or access codes, and I never have to wait for someone to return my page. I didn't even have to worry about Y2K, because there's no computer chip linking me to him.

Just a weathered, bloodstained cross.

No modem, outlet, or batteries required.

It doesn't get any simpler than this.

We need an ever-increasing array of gizmos to stay in touch with our world.

Staying in touch with our God is another story.

Maybe I need to take a moment and unplug. Maybe I'm overdue for an old-fashioned heart-to-heart with the Creator of my soul. My e-mails, cell phone, faxes, and modem aren't going anywhere. They'll still be waiting for me, blinking and beeping for my attention, when I'm through.

And speaking of e-mails, send me one, okay? I always love hearing from readers.

Particularly if they know how to get tire tread marks off a mouse.

3

Common Treasures

YESTERDAY MY FIVE-YEAR-OLD CAME RUNNING in the front door, her face beaming.

"Mom!" Kacie shouted. "I found a treasure!"

She stuck out her fist and, practically bursting at the seams with excitement, began to uncurl her fingers. I expected to see something shiny or uncommon or valuable.

It was the cap of a pen.

Some of Kacie's other treasures include a jar of plastic spiders and a dehydrated gecko she makes me keep in a Ziploc bag on top of the refrigerator.

They say one woman's junk is another woman's treasure. This is particularly true when the second woman is a preschooler.

Of course, I guess I'm not all that different. I love to hunt for treasure, and it doesn't matter if that treasure is someone else's discard or not. Some of my best "treasures" have been unearthed at garage sales, where, for mere pocket change, I've rescued invaluable artifacts from a destiny of dust and neglect or—even worse—a trip to the dump.

One of my more prized garage sale finds is a gold-leafed armadillo. Not to mention the set of porcelain mugs designed to look like pig snouts when raised to the lips of unsuspecting guests.

Sometimes I treasure something because I can see that it has potential. At face value, something can look like a piece of junk, but when observed through the lens of imagination, it takes on newfound grandeur.

Like the brass urn a man tried to sell me at a garage sale. I declined and started to walk away, then hesitated. "You know," I said, thinking aloud as I studied the urn one more time, "drill a couple holes and run some wires and hardware up through the center, and you could turn this into a really classy lamp."

Having talked myself into the purchase, I reached for my wallet.

"No way," the man shook his head and clasped the urn to his chest. "It *would* make a terrific lamp. Sorry, lady, it's not for sale!"

If you and I ever go garage sale-ing together, remind me to keep my mouth shut during high-level negotiations.

Of course, there are other times you can't get someone else to see the value of a "treasure" to save your life.

Just last month, for example, my family was roaming the fall festival in our little town. Spotting a dog-eared copy of *Watership Down* at a used-book table, I tried to contain my ecstasy as I showed my find to my fourteen-year-old daughter. "Oh Kaitlyn! I LOVED this book when I was your age! It's the BEST story! You've GOT to read this book!"

She appeared vaguely interested. "What's it about?"

I gushed, "It's about rabbits."

"Rabbits," she said dryly, raising one eyebrow and giving me a look that teetered somewhere on the continuum between disbelief and disgust.

Just then the associate pastor at our church, Scott Ward, ambled past us with his sons. Stopping to chat, he spotted the book in my hand. "That's a GREAT book," he said enthusiastically. "I remember reading it in school. You should read it, Kaitlyn, it's a really cool story."

Realizing I had failed miserably at conveying to Kaitlyn the rich character development and complex plot of this classic novel, I seized this new opportunity with enthusiasm. "Tell her, Scott," I urged. "Tell her what it's about."

He turned to Kaitlyn, and I watched his face as he searched for just the right words: "It's about . . . rabbits."

Kaitlyn smiled politely, but her eyes said volumes. They were saying, "When I'm their age I hope someone reminds me to take my medication before I go out in public."

I'm learning that while one woman's junk is another woman's treasure, the reverse can also be true: One woman's treasure can be another woman's junk. Unfortunately, this is virtually guaranteed if the second woman is a teenager and the first woman is her mom.

My friend Jeanette recently sent me an e-mail. In it she wrote these words of encouragement: "Karen, you're such a treasure."

At first glance, her words seemed strange. A treasure? Me? Yeah, right! Aren't treasures supposed to be shiny or uncommon or useful? Truth is, some days I feel about as shiny as a dog-eared book, about as uncommon as the cap of a pen, and not nearly as useful as a gold-leafed armadillo (which happens to make a great doorstop, by the way!).

But maybe that's okay. Maybe treasure, like beauty, is in the eye of the beholder. And if my limited imagination can find potential in something as temporal as a brass urn, think what kind of potential God's unlimited imagination can see in you and me!

Someone treasures us.

This is a comforting thought, particularly on days when we don't feel particularly treasured, days we feel overworked, overcommitted, or underappreciated. You know, maybe it would help to have a reminder. A visual aid of sorts. Some common item that, on the surface, appears quite ordinary, yet has been turned by love into a cherished treasure.

A dehydrated gecko works for me.

4

The Best-Laid Plans

As we approach Thanksgiving, many of my friends are busy planning holiday dinners for their families. I tend to run behind on these things. I'm not thinking about Thanksgiving yet. How can I? I'm not done sewing the finishing touches on my five-year-old's Halloween costume.

The truth is, planning far enough in advance to defrost a pound of hamburger in time for dinner is a challenge for me. And when it comes to planning ahead for major holidays . . . well, I can't tell you how many turkeys I've defrosted in less than two hours using a blow-dryer.

But it's not like I NEVER plan ahead.

For example, there was the time I spent hours drawing up plans for a playhouse for our backyard. I used transparent overlays for various construction phases, colored pencils to indicate different building materials, and a black marker to pinpoint every nail. The good news is that my architectural masterpiece has been put to good use. In fact, this very moment it's under my coffee cup, protecting the wood grain of my desk.

Then there was the time I planned to lose thirty pounds before summer. I lost five and discovered that you can really perk up the flavor of fat-free cookies with the simple addition of two scoops of Dreyers Rocky Road ice cream.

I have lots of really great plans. Sometimes I sit around and try to figure out what keeps me from turning a few more of them into reality.

Part of the problem is that I procrastinate.

For example, at this very moment, across from the desk where I'm writing, there is an empty wooden frame hanging on the wall. I hung it there with every intention of putting a picture in it the next day. That was two years ago.

I've heard there are support groups for this kind of thing. I keep meaning to find one.

My other problem is that I get distracted a lot. Like just now. I was busy writing this chapter when I decided I wanted to include a quote by Albert Einstein, something about the power of the imagination. Realizing the book containing the quote was in my bedroom, I ran upstairs. While I was upstairs, my husband phoned to remind me of our lunch plans. Thinking of lunch, I decided to take a quick shower and change clothes. After I showered and dressed, I walked back into my office and sat at my computer and remembered the book. It was still in my bedroom.

Refusing to be undone, I headed back upstairs, thinking, "When I come back down I should bring the vacuum since the dog has been shedding in the den." I went directly to the closet, grabbed the vacuum, wrestled it down the stairs, deposited it in the den, then returned to my desk. It wasn't until I sat down and faced my computer that I remembered the book. Still in my bedroom. Still upstairs.

You'll just take my word about that quote. It was a good one.

And when I'm not forgetting to plan . . . or making a plan and then putting it off . . . or making plans and then getting distracted, I'm having my life planned out for me by my kids.

Which may not be such a bad thing.

One morning when Kacie was four, I was getting her dressed when she said, "Mom, if you worked at a circus, could you take me to work with you?"

"Sure. I'm sure I could arrange that."

"Then stop writing. You need to work for a circus. Can you buy a job at a circus?"

I laughed. "Not exactly. But maybe we could find some reason for them to hire me. I know, I could feed the animals! Wanna help me feed the animals?"

"Okay. But not the lions. Only the nice animals. Like the goats."

Of course. After all, what circus would be complete without goats?

So Kacie has my career all planned out for me. And to tell the truth, it's a nice feeling.

You know who else is in the process of making plans for me and for you as well? I'll give you a hint. He's the author of these powerful words: "For I know the plans I have for you, plans to prosper you and not to harm you, plans to give you hope and a future" (Jer. 29:11).

It's so easy to rush about in a self-induced lather! Indeed, a hefty chunk of my life is spent making plans, breaking plans, and recovering from plans of mine that have gone awry. Perhaps I'd do well to remember that, ultimately, my well-being rests not in the plans of my making, but in the hands of my Maker. Best yet, his plans for me are better than mine could ever be!

Of course, I'm not saying you and I should NEVER make plans. After all, as I write this, Thanksgiving is merely days away and those turkeys don't exactly defrost themselves.

This year, I think I'm going to change my ways. No more last-minute scrambling for me. I'm actually going to plan ahead.

I've already moved my blow-dryer into the kitchen.

5

More Than Meets the Eye

MY GRANDMOTHER HAS A MISCHIEVOUS SIDE.

When my daughter Kacie was, oh, maybe fourteen months old, Mamaw taught her a game. Whenever Mamaw said, "Kacie, pat Mamaw's baby on the head," Kacie would pat herself on the head.

This was cute. Cute and harmless. Then came the summer day we were all sitting on my parents' patio eating grilled chicken, coleslaw, and mashed potatoes.

Kacie was sitting in her high chair, feeding herself with her hands. She'd been working on the mashed potatoes and her hands were covered with the stuff. It looked like she'd been playing in plaster of paris. It looked like she was wearing lumpy gloves. Which is exactly the moment when Mamaw leaned across the table and said . . .

You guessed it.

I was washing mashed potatoes out of Kacie's hair for a week. Five years ago on that summer day Mamaw was feeling her oats. Today she's figuring out how to live with Alzheimer's. She recently moved to a new home, one where many of the other residents have Alzheimer's too, one staffed up to handle the special needs of their guests.

Mamaw's pretty much blind now, but that hasn't stopped her from seeing a dog in her room the past couple months. She's the only one who can see it, but she doesn't seem to realize this because she continues to ask every nurse or visitor the same questions: "Do you see that dog in the corner? Is that your dog?"

Everybody gives her the same answer. Everybody tells her the dog's not there.

One day my folks were visiting Mamaw when another resident wandered in to say hello. George is a weathered Black man with grizzled gray hair and a hundred-watt grin. George greeted Mamaw.

Mamaw said, "George, do you see that dog in the corner? Is that your dog?"

George said, "Nope."

Mamaw's face fell. "You don't see 'im either?"

George said, "I see him all right, but that's not my dog."

A few weeks later, over the phone, my sister Michelle and I were talking about this incident, both of us loving George for the gift he had unwittingly given Mamaw that day, when suddenly there was a long pause and Michelle said:

"What if there's really a dog?"

I said, "What?"

"You know, a dog. For real. What if the rest of us are the crazy ones? What if Mamaw and George are onto something?"

We laughed, but I think there's a part of both of us that hopes it's true.

An alternative reality. One that only the most fragile among us are, somehow, prepared to see. Wow.

Maybe it's not such a Stephen-King concept after all.

The Bible, in fact, talks about just such a reality, a zone, a kingdom actually, where the fragile among us—the poor and the hungry and the tearful—are onto something. Jesus told us that the fragile are onto something because these are the folks who will inherit the kingdom, experience satisfaction, embrace laughter. He says it in the Book of Luke, in chapter six, in what's known as the Beatitudes.

Not that this should surprise us. The whole Bible is filled with glimpses of an alternative reality, a reality that pretty much runs counter to every thing our culture says and believes.

The world says, "Gimme." Jesus says, "Give."

The world says, "Take revenge." Jesus says, "Turn the other cheek."

The world says, "Might makes right." Jesus says, "When you're weak, I'm strong."

The world says, "You can't have enough." Jesus says, "My grace is sufficient for you."

The world says, "Better watch out. God's gonna getcha." Jesus says, "I come to give you abundant life."

The world says, "God is dead. Angels we can handle, crystals we can handle, but God is dead." Jesus says, "I am."

The world doesn't have a clue. Sometimes the things that cause worldly wise folk to roll their eyes turn out to be the truest things of all.

Mamaw'll probably make it to heaven before me, but when I pass through the pearly gates and she and I are strolling those golden streets, there's lots of stuff I think I'll ask her. A citizen of heaven with a good sense of humor and roughly ninety earth-years of faith under her belt, she'll be a wealth of information.

Besides, I'd kinda like to know about the dog.

6

Shop 'Til You Drop

WE'VE JUST SURVIVED the busiest shopping day of the year.

Of course, I'm using the word "we" loosely, referring to American womankind in general. This is because braving the mall on the day after Thanksgiving ranks somewhere, on my personal list of favorite things to do, between getting a root canal and fishing a toddler's favorite stuffed animal out of the toilet.

I know that some women thrive on mass shopping frenzies, but I'm not one of them. Maybe it's because I usually begin the day thinking I'm one of the sharks and end up feeling more like the bait.

I'm convinced there are spiritual grounds for not going shopping the day after Thanksgiving. After all, isn't there a verse somewhere that promises rest for those who have labored and are heavy laden? By the time Thanksgiving is over, I've not only labored hard, but I'm feeling pretty heavily laden with all the stuffing and pumpkin pie I've just consumed. I feel like I've earned a rest. I am not inclined to wake up at daybreak on Friday morning with an insatiable desire to haul my tired, bloated body through hordes of crazed holiday shoppers.

Oh sure, once in awhile I find myself feeling seduced by the notion of saving money at all the first big Christmas sales, but I've learned how to resist temptation. My strategy for getting safely through the Nation's Favorite Shopping Day is to put my credit cards and car keys under lock and key—and then swallow the key. This means there's no possible way I can answer the call of the mall until sometime the following morning or after a trip to the emergency room, whichever occurs first.

I realize I'm missing out on some really good sales.

But think of all the money I'm saving on stress therapy.

Of course, Christmas shopping is stressful even without the crowds. This is because it requires finding The Perfect Gift for roughly four dozen family members, intimate friends, business associates, acquaintances and near strangers, not to mention the couple that has been sending fruitcake for years despite the fact you have no earthly idea where you met them or who they are.

Sometimes I long for a good old-fashioned Walton Christmas. You know, the kind where you give someone an apple or wooden whistle and they go into cardiac arrest from sheer ecstasy.

Of course, I can't say for certain which is the more difficult task: Finding The Perfect Gift for friends and family . . . or dropping hints to help my husband shop for me.

One year for our anniversary Larry bought me a nightgown. You're probably thinking, *So far so good . . .*

He bought it from The Disney Store.

The front of the gown featured a life-sized illustration of Rafiki. (Just in case you don't have children, or you have children but have spent the past five years living on Mars, Rafiki is the wizened old baboon guru in the Disney movie *The Lion King.*)

But perhaps the most intriguing part of the gift was the matching pair of socks that looked like baboon feet.

Now, if the love of your life has never given you a pair of knitted baboon feet, you probably don't know the true meaning of the phrase "Academy Award–winning performance." I'll bet Meryl Streep couldn't have feigned a more convincing performance of ecstatic gratitude, although I think I could have gushed far more convincingly over just about anything else, including an apple or a wooden whistle.

In other words, I tried to appear grateful, but I don't think I did a very good job because Larry figured out right away that I wasn't too crazy about the gift. He's pretty astute about these things. Of course, it's possible that I tipped him off. I think it happened right after I opened the box, right about the moment I blurted, "Ahh . . . I hope you kept the receipt."

Okay, so maybe I'm an ingrate. Apparently I not only keep my eyes peeled for The Perfect Gift when I'm shopping for my friends and family, but I also look for it when unwrapping presents addressed to me.

Maybe I'm looking in the wrong place.

The Bible tells me that "every good and perfect gift comes from above."

Oh, sure, I'll be the first to admit that the Lord has sent a few things into my life that I'd love to return. There are times I take an initial look and blurt, "Ahh, God, I hope you kept the receipt . . ." But hindsight usually shows me that what he gave was exactly what I needed after all. There are even a few gifts that I suspect will require the kind of hindsight I can only get in heaven. Who knows? Those might turn out to be the most perfect gifts of all.

I'm learning to trust the Giver, even when I don't always understand the gifts.

Most of the time, however, the gifts he gives exceed my wildest hopes and dreams.

The fact is that God's gifts—unlike the purchases of harried Christmas shoppers, well-meaning husbands, and other mere mortals—are never the wrong size, color, or pattern. It'll be interesting to see what gifts he has in store for me this coming year. Although I don't mind admitting that, if I have my druthers, baboon socks won't be anywhere on the list.

7

It's Beginning to feel a Lot like christmas

DECEMBER IS UPON US, which means it's that festive time of year when the word "traditions" really means something, when it takes on entire new levels of significance, when merely saying the word conjures a broad spectrum of images and emotions.

Two examples that come immediately to mind are "stress" and "guilt."

Not that stress and guilt can't be festive. They can be. In fact, we probably wouldn't recognize Christmas without them.

Indeed, if we had a completely stress-and-guilt-free Christmas, my guess is that somewhere mid-January we'd find ourselves asking: "Did we even celebrate Christmas last month? I remember a flawless dinner and beautifully wrapped presents and well-behaved relatives, but for some reason it just didn't FEEL like Christmas. Something was missing, but I can't seem to put my finger on it."

Of course, it's possible that everything would feel more normal as soon as we got our credit card bill in the mail or discovered those holiday pounds reflected on our bathroom scales. At that point, we'd undoubtedly burst into a rousing rendition of "Jingle Bells" as a result of all that new-found Christmas spirit suddenly welling up inside of us.

The weird thing about stress and guilt is that, even though they tend to arrive hand in hand, they come from completely opposite sources. We feel stressed because we're doing too much, and guilty because we think we're somehow not doing enough. You'd think they would somehow cancel each other out, wouldn't you? (Of course, I used to think the same thing about drinking Diet Coke with pepperoni pizza, or adding fat-free ice cream to pecan pie. Oh well. Live and learn!)

Naturally, there are other Christmas traditions besides stress and guilt. Take baking, for example. One of my traditions is to make Christmas cookies from an old family recipe.

My other tradition is to lose the recipe.

To date, my mother has given me the recipe on at least nine different occasions, sometimes more than once for the same holiday.

Another favorite holiday tradition is sending cards. For three years running I kept the tradition of writing a Christmas newsletter, addressing dozens of envelopes to family and friends, and then letting the whole project sit on the den coffee table until March. Two years ago I finally gave up the dream of sending Christmas greetings to loved ones. Of course, I still experience guilt at not keeping in touch, but at least I can take the time I once spent addressing envelopes and use it for something more constructive. Like calling my mom for that cookie recipe.

In theory, I think traditions are a great idea. After all, there's nothing I'd love better than to lovingly, year after year, craft a Martha Stewart Christmas for my family, complete with beloved traditions that seem to glow with a rich patina bestowed by the passage of time.

In reality, however, traditions are a bit more complicated. They are complicated because they require a lot of planning ("Let me check my calendar") . . . props ("Has anybody seen the box with the Christmas decorations?) . . . and cooperation from family members ("What do you mean you have a date with Jason on the night of our Annual Christmas Caroling Extravaganza!?!").

Of course, I'm not saying we shouldn't strive to create meaningful traditions for loved ones.

I'm just saying we shouldn't beat ourselves up when our "Martha Stewart Christmas" turns out more akin to "Holiday Mayhem with Larry, Moe, and Curly."

We shouldn't beat up our friends and family over it, either.

How do we know we're taking this tradition thing a little too seriously? I think a big clue for me is when I hear myself bark the following phrase to my kids: "I realize your legs are going numb, but no, you cannot leave the kitchen table. There are still twelve dozen cookies left to decorate, and we're going to sit here and have fun and create a warm memory by decorating every last one of them whether you like it or not!"

You know, there's a great story in the Bible that says a lot to me each December. It's found in the Book of Mark, where Jesus' disciples were criticized for "harvesting" on the Sabbath because they ate a few wheat grains while walking through a field. Jesus responded to the criticism by reminding everyone that "the Sabbath was made for man, and not man for the Sabbath."

Likewise, I try to remind myself that holiday traditions are here to serve me and my loved ones, not the other way around. I never want to compromise peace of mind or harmony in relationships for any given tradition.

Relationships, after all, are more important than ritual.

This is great news. Getting my priorities straight certainly relieves a lot of the pressure I tend to put on myself during the holidays. In fact, in honor of my new commitment to put relationships over ritual, I think I'll call someone I care about for no other reason than to say "Hi" and "I love you." I could call one of my girlfriends . . . or either of my sisters . . . or—I know—my mom. I think I'll call my mother.

I needed to call her anyway. I'm going to a Christmas potluck this weekend, and I've been asked to bring the cookies.

8

Name That Tune

I LOVE TO SING. I couldn't sing my way out of a paper bag, but I still love to sing. And since I have yet to be held hostage in a paper sack for lack of a song, I'm confident that even though my warbling deficiency may be annoying, it is hardly life threatening.

Especially at Christmastime. Everybody sings at Christmas whether they can carry a tune or not. Christmas hymns, songs, and jingles fill the air. Even animals get in the act. Indeed, the Chipmunks' *Christmas Album* remains a holiday best-seller, and even the "Jingle Bells" barking dogs have gone on to develop their talent. I hear they're doing Handel's *Messiah* this year.

So I've been thinking about Christmas carols.

Actually, I've been thinking about some of the lyrics of Christmas carols.

I realize that thinking deeply about the lyrics of songs we love is not exactly necessary, and sometimes it isn't even advisable. After all, some very beloved songs have hit the top of the charts and enjoyed huge financial success despite the fact that they contain lyrics that, if you study their Latin roots, appear to have been written by blondes. (And if you think I'm blonde-bashing, think again—these savvy women are bizillionaires by now. They have not only amassed tons of songwriting revenue, but think of all the royalties from those blonde jokes they've been ghostwriting for years!)

Look at any genre of music and you can find double-take lyrics, phrases that demand a second listen despite the fact—or maybe because of the fact—that they don't make a whole lot of sense. Remember the song "Witch Doctor" by David Seville? Trust me when I say that more immortal lyrics beginning with the phrase, "Oo ee oo ah ah" have not been penned in our generation or any other.

But we're talking about Christmas carols here. The main problem with Christmas carols tends to be, not that they were written by savvy blondes, but that they were written, most of them anyway, by Joe Isuzu.

Certainly you remember Joe, the former spokesperson for Isuzu automobiles. He made Jim Carey's truth-impaired character in *Liar, Liar* look like Honest Abe in comparison. When it came to Joe, the reality check was in the mail. And even after it arrived, it bounced. Many people thought the clever ad campaign featuring this reality-challenged spokesman was a spoof. I'm not so sure. I have reason to believe that before he got a job peddling cars, Joe eked out a living by writing many of our Christmas carols.

How else could we end up with lyrics like, "All I want for Christmas is my two front teeth"?

This is obviously a lie.

The truth is that children will NOT settle for their own teeth for Christmas. Neither are they satisfied with oranges in their stockings or an American Flyer wagon as their coveted single gift. No, today's children want the moon, creating holiday wish lists that require not only a table of contents but thumb tabs as well.

I also have to wonder about the phrase "All is calm, all is bright." It may have applied the night Jesus was born, but Christmas at my house is anything but calm. Between baking cookies, hunting for white-elephant gifts, hosting the neighborhood cookie exchange, shopping, assembling the artificial Christmas tree (and wondering why there are four branches left over), sewing Christmas pageant costumes, and writing the family holiday newsletter, it's not unusual for me to find that the word "calm" has been deleted from my vocabulary. It has, in fact, been replaced with words and phrases like "Rolaids," "nervous tic," and "I NEED CHOCOLATE AND I NEED IT NOW."

Now, "Laughing as we go, HA HA HA!" isn't bad. Maybe Joe had help with this one. Maybe from Jim Carey. Because laughter isn't a bad way to approach the holidays. Sometimes, when the season takes a particularly chaotic turn, it's best to throw up your hands and laugh about it. Did you burn the snowball cookies? Forget where you parked your car at the mall? Get your Christmas cards in the mail the day before Washington's birthday? Then take two belly laughs and call me in the morning. The truth is, laughter reduces stress, pumps up the immune system, diffuses squabbles, lifts the spirits, broadens the perspective, and feels great. Best yet, it has no calories and can't make you pregnant. Feeling stressed? Don't buckle. Chuckle instead!

There's another song that comes to mind, and I really hope Joe didn't write this one, because I want it to be true. The words are, "Let every heart prepare him room."

Unfortunately, sometimes I think we put more effort into making room in our refrigerators for Christmas dinner leftovers than we spend preparing room in our hearts for Christ.

Maybe this year can be different. Since we've still got a couple weeks until Christmas, perhaps we can begin today to give Jesus a more prominent role in our celebrations. How? I know, for me, an attitude of gratitude does wonders. Am I shopping for loved ones? Baking cookies? Entertaining holiday guests? What if I thought of every task—every tradition, every labor of love—as a token of my gratitude? An act of thankful worship of the Christ whose birth we celebrate each year?

There's another song, and I think the lyrics say it well: "Oh, come let us adore him." It's sage advice, written by someone with not only a nice sense of rhythm, but biblical priorities and no small measure of wisdom.

I'd be willing to bet it was a blonde.

9

Christmas, a Labor of Love

I DON'T KNOW WHY **S**ANTA GETS ALL THE CREDIT.

After all, what family do you know in real life where the man of the house is the driving force responsible for making Christmas happen? I can't think of many. The truth is, we women carry the lion's share of the responsibility—and the privilege—of creating memorable holidays for the folks we love.

I think women shoulder the bulk of the work because a successful Christmas requires skills that come more naturally to women than to men.

Like spending massive sums of money.

And that's just for starters. Women are also better at manipulating unwieldy pieces of wrapping paper, as well as knowing the behind-the-scenes politics of all our friends so that uncomfortable combinations of people don't show up at the same Christmas party. We're also ahead when it comes to remembering the correct spelling of the names of people on our gift list, including distant relatives, bosses and coworkers, children's teachers, and even our own children. (And I only say this because, several weeks after my daughter Kaitlyn was born, I overheard her dad misspelling her name to a well-wisher on the phone!)

Pulling off the perfect Christmas also requires an understanding of the nuances of giblet gravy, an ability to whip up an angel costume in twenty minutes or less, and a mastery of the perfect pie crust. (My secret? After I remove the pie crust from the freezer, I make sure I peel off the cellophane and cardboard label before pouring in the filling.)

Women have these skills. Men don't.

This is why you can't convince me that Mrs. Claus isn't the unsung hero. Don't tell me she's not behind the scenes, coaching her husband every step of the way. I can hear her now, peering over his shoulder as he makes out the gift list: "Santa, honey, don't even THINK about giving that new garage door remote to newlywed Mrs. Jones. She's going to be much happier with the perfume. Trust me."

I can see her following him to the sled with last-minute shopping instructions: "Target has special holiday hours, so you don't have to rush. There's a sale on Pokémon backpacks at Sears, and whatever you do, DON'T go to Bath World—this is Wednesday and senior citizens get a 10 percent discount, so the place will be crowded and you won't be able to maneuver the aisles for the walkers. Did you remember the list? Your wallet? Good. And if I'm not here when you get home, the Scotch tape is in the top left desk drawer, and wrapping paper's in the hall closet."

I can even hear her coaching her husband as he's getting dressed on Christmas Eve: "I don't care if anyone sees you or not. The black dress socks and baseball cap are tacky. Wear something else. And don't try to tell me your red suit is dirty, because I picked it up from the cleaners just this morning."

If you're like me, you take your role as Christmas-maker very seriously. Indeed, Christmas is upon us and right about now you and I are toting lists of about two million last-minute things that need doin' before December 25th. It's not that men and kids don't help with the planning, shopping, cooking, and decorating but, if women were removed from the picture, Christmas dinners would include tater tots and two out of three gifts would come from Home Depot.

Christmas depends on us, ladies. The success of the coming holiday is on our shoulders.

Yes, women make Christmas.

It's our labor of love.

Which makes me think of another woman, a woman for whom Christmas was a labor of love in a very real sense of the word.

Because a long time ago, there was a woman who held Christmas, not on her shoulders, but in her arms. Like you and me, she had the privilege of shaping Christmas, but it wasn't through the labor of her hands. Indeed, Christmas entered the world through the painful rending of her pregnant body, and then she held him in her arms as he slept.

As I'm rushing through the last hectic days before Christmas, it's not a bad time to remember that, as well-intentioned as they may be, my efforts don't "make" Christmas. God did that—through Mary—2,000 years ago. Which makes Christmas complete and perfect, just the way it is.

If I have any goal this December, maybe it should be to celebrate Christmas the way Mary did: By embracing the person called the Christ.

Well, that . . . and staying away from Bath World on Wednesdays.

10

The Christmas Babies

A PORTION OF THIS COLUMN IS FOURTEEN YEARS OLD.
This is because I am including in these pages a letter I wrote
to my daughter Kaitlyn in honor of our first Christmas together. She was six weeks old at the time.

The letter has never been published.

Oh, I tried to share it with friends and family one year, but
there was a minor complication. Remember how, in an earlier chapter, I confessed that I'm such a procrastinator I've
been known to write Christmas cards, address them to friends
and family, then let the pile of envelopes sit on my den coffee
table for months on end?

Well, back in '91, a copy of this letter was in each of eighty
Christmas cards that eventually ended up in the trash. They

ended up in the trash because it was May, and I needed the space on the coffee table to write out valentines.

Christmas is upon us and right about now you and I have To-Do lists that are a mile long. If you're like me, you'll get a lot of things done. And if you're REALLY like me, there'll be more than a few things on your list that you'll never actually accomplish. The good news is that life will go on. You'll discover that just because you didn't finish your To-Do list, it's not the end of the world as we know it. (Although if for some reason the world-as-we-know-it comes to a crashing halt on December 26, I may have to reconsider that last statement.)

It's amazing all the things that need to be done in the last days before Christmas. Even things that don't have anything to do with Christmas suddenly need to be done before Christmas. Like fixing the braided rug in my office. The threads holding the braids in a spiral have been unraveling for months, but for some unexplained, masochistic reason it didn't feel life-threatening until NOW, one week before Christmas, when I'm so stressed and busy that I don't even have time to wash my hair and shave my legs during the same shower.

Naturally, this is when I found myself looking at the rug in a crazed panic and thinking, "That rug must be repaired and it must be repaired TODAY."

This is why I was willing to try The Shortcut.

So this morning I bypassed the needle and thread and went straight for the hot glue gun.

Actually, it worked great. The rug looks like new. Of course, I'm wondering if I was as careful as I should have been. I say this because our German shepherd walked across the rug as I was working, and he hasn't moved since.

But my point is that you and I have a lot to do right now and a lot on our minds as well.

Which is why I decided to include the following letter. It's about another woman who had a lot on her mind as well, some 2000 Christmases ago.

So here they are, fresh from mothballs, the words I penned to my own baby fourteen years ago. Consider them my Christmas gift to you, a small token from one harried woman to another. Merry Christmas to you and yours!

☆ ☆ ☆

Dearest Kaitlyn,
Tonight I put the finishing touches on the Christmas tree—silver ribbon and a garland of red wooden beads. Then I cradled you in my arms and turned on the lights, convinced the smile that appeared on your face was from delight and not by coincidence.

And I couldn't help but think of another Christmas baby, born long ago to a mother who must have shared my enchantment with the miracle of birth.

Did she, I wondered, interpret every smile as an intimate communication, as I do now?

Did she spend hours memorizing a tiny face, searching infant eyes with her own, caressing soft round cheeks?

I picture that mother kissing sweet, rosebud lips, as I do yours. And she must have traced the curve of a turned-up nose a thousand times.

Did that mother, while cradling her baby to her breast, whisper promises and secrets, hopes and dreams? Did she tell her son—as I tell you—about sunsets and holidays, puppies and stars? Did she describe for him his earthly father? Did she tell him about God?

How she must have marveled at the grasp of five tiny fingers curled around her own and considered what wonders this infant being would accomplish when he grew tall. And as she did, did she ever whisper hopes about his future? Did she whisper promises from her past?

And when she looked down at a chubby face relaxed in sleep—with lips parted and tiny lashes resting gently on rosy cheeks—perhaps she thought about how very soon her baby would be grown and gone. And perhaps, like me, she let the tears well up in her eyes, trace a pattern down her face, and splash unhindered on a chubby hand.

This year, I have my own precious Christmas baby. And I understand, better than ever before, a mother's love for a Christmas baby long ago.

And when you are old enough to understand, I'll tell you all about that mother's baby. And I'll tell you what she couldn't have known as she swaddled, nursed, and loved him: that one day her baby would die so that mine might live. So that you might live. And of all the Christmas blessings today or yesterday, this is the greatest by far.

11

Cold Weather Sports

IT'S COLD OUTSIDE.

I know it's cold outside because I happen to be visiting my folks in Colorado and, as I look out the window, I can see snow on the ground. Even back home in Texas, I hear they've had an unexpected cold spell and that the temperature's been down to twenty degrees.

When it gets chilly like this, it's only natural to find ourselves thinking about cold weather sports.

Such as applying moisterizer.

If you ask me, the Olympics should recognize moisturizer application as a winter sport and allow women to compete internationally. I just can't decide whether the competition should be based on speed or results. Should the gold go to the woman who can apply the most lotion in the least amount of time or to the woman who goes home baby-bottom-soft after beginning the week most resembling a Gila monster?

Other cold weather sports? Scraping ice off a frozen windshield is always a riveting event. So is hunting for a preschooler's missing mitten. And speaking of lost mittens, I'm waiting for a forward-thinking company to come up with telephone-activated locating devices that can be attached to mittens, blankies, even pacifiers. That way, when Junior is screaming at the top of his lungs for the saliva-stained blankie that has gone suddenly AWOL, you could walk to the phone, dial a number, and listen around the house for the responding beep. I'd buy a dozen such devices and attach them to all sorts of things that I can't afford to lose: My car keys would be prime candidates. My five-year-old's mittens could benefit as well. I'd even be willing to attach one to my bottle of moisturizer.

Another popular cold weather sport is trying to keep the house warm. This sport requires good manual dexterity as well as a high tolerance for emotional pain. This is because it usually involves writing checks to utility companies for obscene sums of money.

I remember one December when our heater went out. I called around, but no one could come out to fix it for several days. Larry and I tried to look on the bright side. We figured we'd save a little money on the electric bill that month. The bad news is that we were in the middle of a cold spell.

We did everything we could to stay warm, including relying on the kinds of gritty survival skills my husband perfected during his years as an Eagle Scout.

We built a fire.

Ah, but this was no ordinary fire.

After creating an architectural masterpiece of kindling and logs that would have garnered an approving nod from the most stringent Scout Master, my husband decided to get innovative. He collected palms that had fallen from the palm tree in front of our house, certain that the massive brittle fans would provide excellent fuel.

And he was right. He tossed a few into the fireplace, and they immediately burst into flames. Indeed, the fire roared hot and ferocious, with long flames leaping out of the fireplace, licking their way toward the mantel and singeing the toes out of all the Christmas stockings.

As black smoke began pouring into the house, Larry and I looked at each other and said, at the exact same moment, two little words. Savvy Eagle Scouts rarely have to say these words to each other, mainly because savvy-er Scout Masters only let them build fires in the woods.

We said in unison: "The flue!"

Indeed, the fireplace flue was firmly closed. The good news is that Larry eventually found a crowbar, reached in through the flames, and opened the flue. The bad news is that, to get rid of all the smoke in the house, we had to open all the windows for several hours, which meant the temperature in our house dropped even further, and we were forced to devise new ways to keep warm.

Kaitlyn was born nine months later.

This, of course, suggests a whole new category of cold weather sports. In fact, anyone who remembers the last Winter Olympics remembers that many commentators reported a disappointing drop in viewer interest. My guess is that the inclusion of this kind of sport would go a long way toward reviving interest and boosting viewer ratings.

But I shouldn't complain about winter. I shouldn't complain about any season, really, because every season says something to us about the kind of Being who would create such masterpieces as snowflakes, tender spring growth, summer thunderstorms, and fall's rich harvest.

I hadn't looked at a snowflake—I mean really looked at a snowflake—in years. But I did this week, with my kids, as we were playing in the snow. And when I studied the intricate design, exquisite even as it melted into my glove, I was filled with awe. "God made this," I told Kacie. She was clearly moved, taking the opportunity of my reflective pause to plant a fistful of wet snow in my face.

Not that I mind a little snow in the face. In fact, harsh elements don't worry me a bit. I am, after all, a serious athlete, well-practiced in my chosen sport.

Just give me a bottle of Jergens, and I'll bring home the gold every time.

12

The Secret
to Foolproof Resolutions

IT'S THE BEGINNING OF A NEW YEAR, which means it's time once again to take stock and identify changes that will make me a better person and improve the quality of my life.

I've decided to save time this year. Rather than start from scratch making my list of resolutions, I'm just going to dust off last year's list. I can do this because the same goals tend to show up year after year. For example, every single year, my list begins as follows:

Resolution Number One: Never eat anything again for the rest of my life.

I read somewhere that in the weeks between Thanksgiving and Christmas, each American gains an average of seven pounds. This tells me an awful lot of people actually lose weight over the holidays. I say this because my holiday weight gain tends to be in the triple-digit category, which means in order to end up with a national average of only seven pounds per person, some folks somewhere are dropping pounds big time.

The worst part about New Year's resolutions is that they are so short-lived. My wedding night negligee lasted longer than the majority of the promises I've made to myself on various January firsts throughout the years.

But I think I finally have it figured out.

I think I've finally come up with a surefire way to actually follow through with the resolutions I make this year.

Best yet, I'm going to share my secret with you. In fact, by following my instructions you, too, can wow your friends in April by announcing that you have honored your New Year's resolutions for four whole months with a flawless fervency that even Gandhi would have admired.

My secret is simply this: When you make your New Year's wish list this year, select the kinds of resolutions that you could execute successfully even if you were in a coma.

For example, this year I plan to remove, from my list, the goal of losing twenty pounds. I am going to replace it with a goal that states that no conventions attended by Elvis impersonators will be allowed to convene in my home during any month that ends in the letter *y*.

And you know that resolution that says I will get out of debt by eating out less often, reusing tinfoil, and making homemade Christmas presents out of recycled dryer lint? Well, forget it. I'm going to replace that resolution with something a little more failsafe. In fact, I've been thinking of resolving that I will never, ever allow my children to engage in science fair projects that involve the words "plastic surgery," no matter how much they beg or how many chins I have.

In fact, for even less stress and an even greater chance at success, consider resolutions such as these:

"I promise to air out the sheets on my bed by leaving it unmade whenever I am running late for work."

"I resolve to reduce my intake of sugar and fat whenever I am not currently eating sugar or fat."

"I resolve to end the new year older than I am today."

Sometimes, less is more.

If I were to put a passage from the Bible on my list of New Year's resolutions, what might I choose? I could always pick the Ten Commandments, or even 1 Corinthians 13. There's no doubt about it—these verses would certainly make worthy resolutions.

But if less is more, the verse I've always loved can be found in Micah, chapter 6, verse 8: "What does the LORD require of you but to do justice, to love kindness, and to walk humbly with your God?" (NASB).

Now there's a resolution that's worth its salt.

Do justice, love kindness, and walk humbly with my Lord.

Okay, I'll be the first to admit this resolution doesn't exactly fit in the category of "things you can accomplish while comatose." But you have to agree that it's not too complex. It's not unreasonable, either. Best yet, it comes with a perk or two. For starters, when I'm having a hard time following through with this resolution, the Holy Spirit is waiting to come to my assistance and help me turn these powerful words into a reality in my life. All I have to do is ask.

And when I stumble completely—when I am downright unjust, mean, and proud—Jesus is waiting to forgive and give grace.

All I have to do is ask.

What a deal!

Every January, I get frustrated because my New Year's resolutions are usually the exact same promises I made to myself the previous year. But if you ask me, these words from Micah deserve to be on my list of resolutions year after year after year.

Right next to the ban on Elvis conventions in my living room.

Spring

13

Meet Walter

I TOOK MY DOG TO THE VET THIS MORNING.

Walter is a white German shepherd puppy, although I use the word *puppy* loosely. This is because Walter slobbers like a fire hydrant. He eats like a vacuum. And when he's not trying to scramble onto my lap like a fifty-pound Pomeranian, he's ricocheting around the house like a loose balloon on amphetamines.

So you can see why, when Walter started moping around the house a few days ago, I knew something was wrong.

I got the prognosis (and the bill) this morning.

Walter has tonsillitis.

I didn't even know dogs had tonsils.

I guess I shouldn't complain. As long as I'm paying a vet bill, at least I'm getting my money's worth. At least tonsillitis is a real ailment, unlike the LAST time Walter had to go to the vet. It was about two months ago, and Walter had just spent three days limping and moaning around the house. I searched for burrs, broken bones, cuts, or bruises to no avail. I was heading out the front door to take Walter to the vet when my teenage daughter said, "Maybe it has something to do with the fact that Kacie's been standing on his leg."

I explained all this to the vet as he was examining my dog. When the exam was through, the good doctor gave me his recommendation: "I'd suggest you tell your five-year-old to stop standing on his leg."

That'll be sixty dollars, please.

But I'm not complaining. Walter is worth it. He adds a lot of value to our home. I can't say how much in terms of dollars yet because I'm still researching the going rate for shed dog hair, but if there's any sort of market for this stuff at all, we could be talking really big bucks.

So I'm doing my best to keep Walter healthy. Actually, that's my goal when it comes to the rest of my family as well. We're going into flu season, and it's time to stock up on cough syrup and decongestant.

Not to mention Vitamin C, veggies, and warm mittens. After all, they say an ounce of prevention is worth a pound of cure. This is why I make my kids button up in cold weather. This is also why I tell them to "brush and floss after meals," "don't run with sharp sticks," and "please stop leaning backwards in that chair right now before you fall and break something or I walk over there and wring your neck, whichever comes first."

But they don't get it. They think they're indestructible. They think I'm being Mrs. Killjoy. But when they get sick or hurt, suddenly I'm NURSE Killjoy and their favorite person in the world.

Not that I mind. I love my girls, and I'm happy to be there when they need me. I just wish they'd listen to me more often. I can't spare them from every virus, bug, or accident, but I sure could steer them clear of more than a few.

Some things, as we've said, are just easier to avoid than fix. Same thing goes for other areas in my kids' lives, and in my life and yours too. Like this one friend of mine. She told me talking to men in chat rooms is just fun, and nothing'll come of it. She didn't know that I thought that too, but that it started leading me down a scary detour. I had to cut through some brambles to get back to the main road, but I'm back where I want to be and wiser for the wear. I told her about it, but she says she's fine. She's in control. She's handling it.

Just like someone else I love. Someone I knew in college. She had it handled too. Just a drink now and then to relax. Now she's downing three or four a night and wondering why she feels so trapped.

Just like another friend. There were a few months at the beginning when her affair felt preventable, not that she tried very hard because, let's face it, it felt pretty good at the moment. Now she's in the fixin' stage, trying to put back the pieces of her life, and she never dreamed it'd be this hard.

Just like you. I don't know the details of your story, but my guess is that you've got one. Something you could have prevented, maybe still can. I have two things to say to you:

First, you're not too late. Getting ahold of whatever is ailing your spirit today—no matter how long it's gone on—is terrific prevention against creating more sorrow for yourself tomorrow.

Second, whenever it is you jump in and say, "This is it! I'm going to get ahold of this attitude/affair/addiction/habit/feud/temptation right now before it goes unchecked another minute!" (whether you say it when you've merely lost control of your thoughts or whether your actions have jumped into the fray as well), one thing doesn't change: You're loved just the same with a passionate love by a holy God.

My friend Linda once told me, "I'm just now realizing how much God loves me, and that there's nothing I can do—NOTHING—that will diminish that love."

I said, "Then why not just live however we want? Why worry about holding back?"

Linda said, "Because I don't want the wounds that sin creates in my life."

Yeah, those wounds. I've had them. They're no fun. And, if you ask me, that's the best reason of all to buy an ounce of prevention. But as for God's love, well, that never wavers. And if I end up needing that pound of cure after all, he loves me even then.

As for Walter, he's feeling much better, thanks for asking. In fact, I'm so stirred up by all this "ounce of prevention" stuff that I've taken a few steps to keep Walter from future ailments.

He didn't seem to mind the vitamins, but trust me when I tell you he's not at all happy about the mittens.

14

clutter Management 101

I'M GETTING THE URGE AGAIN.

It hits me every year. Maybe it's brought on from thumbing through Target ads and seeing all the plastic storage boxes and closet dividers on sale.

But whatever the reason, every January I get this urge to organize my home.

Some years, I'll admit, I take two aspirin and watch reruns of *Sanford and Son* until The Urge goes away (I suspect this is because, compared to their home, mine looks like it belongs between the covers of *Better Homes and Gardens*).

But other years I get really motivated and make an effort to tame the jungle of clutter in my home.

Of course, this is easier said than done. Sometimes I get the feeling my house is a little like the Eagles' Hotel California:

Things check in but they don't check out. (Or is that the Roach Motel? I can never remember!) What kinds of things? How about clothes that haven't been in style since I had to have my pet rock put to sleep, or my collection of Barry Manilow songs—on eight track—or the two dozen plaques I own that try to assure me that "A Messy Desk Is the Sign of a Creative Mind" (all gifts from friends who know me a little too well).

The only good thing about clutter is that, indeed, one woman's junk is another woman's treasure. One month I managed to clean out two closets and hold a garage sale. I made $400. (I figure if I clean out the rest of my closets I can probably put one of my children through college.)

I'm not sure where all the clutter comes from. Oh sure, junk mail is a big chunk of it. Happy Meal toys comprise another large portion. Half-used tubes of abandoned makeup and facial care products are another hefty category. And what about those wire hangers? Have you ever once in your life actually purchased a wire hanger? Me neither. I always buy the plastic tube hangers.

So why, even as we speak, are my closets being held hostage by legions of hostile wire hangers?

I have this theory. I have a theory that while my house looks, on the outside, like a perfectly normal single-family dwelling, there are, in reality, sinister forces at work here. I have reason to believe that my house has been hexed and, as a result, any family who lives within these walls will be forced to contend with the Curse of the Copulating Clutter.

I know this sounds far-fetched, but I don't know quite how else to explain the fact that every morning I wake to twice as much clutter as the night before. The stuff breeds during the midnight hours, I'm certain of it.

What clutter-management techniques have I acquired? Well, sometimes, I try to recycle. Over the holidays, for example, I enlisted the artistic talents of friend Gavin Jones to craft a wire metal hanger into a hat from which a sprig of mistletoe could be hung four inches above the head of the wearer.

But we were lucky. Not every unwanted household item can be recycled into something quite so useful.

Which gives me an idea. I've always had a crush on Richard Dean Anderson in his role as MacGyver. I'm thinking they should produce a reunion show, and tape it at my house. Think of all the useful things MacGyver could invent from the clutter in my home. Why, put him in one room alone, and he could build a space shuttle. Or a minivan. Or best yet, something I could REALLY put to good use, like Rosie, the robotic maid from the Jetsons.

But the tangible clutter in my home isn't the worst of it. Old magazines, mugs featuring pictures of state capitals, a tray of bobbins belonging to the sewing machine I gave to Goodwill seven years ago—these things may be annoying, but they're manageable.

It's the other clutter in my life that I can't quite get a handle on, the stuff even MacGyver can't touch. Stuff like bad habits and old hurts and painful memories, not to mention lingering lusts and dusty grudges and broken dreams.

Stuff I should have gotten rid of a long time ago.

Maybe I should forget Anderson's Hollywood agents and put in a call to Someone who can REALLY help. There is, after all, a Master Recycler, someone who promises that he can take ALL things in my life and make them work out—somehow, if I let him—for good. His awesome lemons-into-lemonade abilities even prompted one Bible hero, Joseph, to look into the eyes of the brothers who betrayed him and admit, "What you meant for evil, God meant for good."

God doesn't recycle overnight. Sometimes he takes years. But I'm realizing that he can't even get started on my clutter until I unclench my fists and hand it over.

What he'll make of it all is up to him.

I know it's not very spiritual, but I'll go ahead and say it anyway:

I'm hoping for at least one Rosie out of the whole mess.

15

Say Good-bye to Good Intentions

I FINALLY DID IT.

I thumbed through the phone book, found the number, dialed it, and made an appointment for two weeks from today.

I'm going to see an electrologist.

I've been meaning to make an appointment for months. Lots of months. Actually, dozens of them. But can you blame me for procrastinating?

You've heard of electrolysis, right? It's a way of getting rid of unwanted hair on your face and body. The way I understand it, I'm paying about a dollar a minute to have a certified technician stick a miniature cattle prod into my hair follicles, then turn to a hunchbacked assistant and shout the words, "Throw the switch!"

I think it also has to be a stormy night.

It's a drastic measure, I know. But you'll have to trust me when I say that I'm not taking this step lightly. I can either submit to these Mary-Shelleyesque electrical treatments, or I can continue resembling Wolfman Jack. It's come down to this.

Actually, I've been battling these two dozen annoying chin hairs for several years now. The final straw occurred this past weekend. We had friends coming over Sunday afternoon to watch a Cowboys game on TV, and I was in the bathroom getting ready, and . . . well . . . I nicked myself shaving.

Not my leg, mind you. My face.

I stemmed the bleeding with a twist of toilet paper and looked at myself in the mirror. I thought, this is what happens to fourteen-year-old boys who borrow their dad's razor for the first time. They look just like this, with toilet paper spit wads on their chins. Of course, fourteen-year-old boys don't wear Caffe Latte lipstick by Estee Lauder, but other than that, the similarities were striking.

It was time to take permanent action.

Even though I haven't had my appointment yet, it feels good to have made the call. There's something about finally getting around to a long-intended project that feels really great.

In fact, I'm so inspired by how good I feel right now that I'm wondering what other loose-end projects I can tackle. What else have I been putting off that I could get out of the way?

Oh. I just remembered one. Okay, I'll admit this one's no fun. In fact, having my follicles electrocuted by a mad scientist ranks higher on my list of favorite activities than this next project.

You probably know what I'm thinking about. In fact, my guess is that you're overdue as well.

I'm thinking about The Dreaded Well-Woman Exam.

Who came up with this process, anyway? I mean, a total stranger tells me to wear nothing but a paper towel, plant my feet in metal stirrups that feel like they've been stored in the freezer, and then I'm supposed to relax and chitchat while he maneuvers a Buick around in there? I don't THINK so.

Sigh.

But it's a necessary evil. I'm going to stop procrastinating and make the call. You should too.

Let's see. What else have I been intending to do? I'm going to make it something fun this time. Oh, I know! Have lunch with Jeffie Burns. She's the Children's Ministry Director at my church, and she's got a wit sharper than an electrolysis needle. Time spent with Jeffie always gets me laughing and leaves me uplifted. We've been promising to "do lunch" for months. I think I'll nail something down.

January seems to be the month for grandiose new schemes and resolutions. But you know what? I'd love to spend it just catching up on old plans and good intentions.

Something else I've always intended to do has been to read through the Bible in a year. In fact, one of the Bibles I have is already divided into 365 readings. I've just never cracked the cover. I'd have to do a little catch-up here at the beginning, but I know it would be an enjoyable journey.

You know, good intentions and a buck'll buy you a cup of coffee. Maybe it's time to turn some of those good intentions into reality.

Wanna join me? Call your OB-GYN. Have lunch with a friend. Dust off your Bible.

And if you've been battling unwanted hairs, take heart. I hear Dr. Frankenstein's available for evening and weekend appointments as well.

16

Crash Diet at Freeway Speeds

I'VE BEEN OFF MY DIET FOR WEEKS.

This morning my breakfast consisted of cookies and potato chips. The good news is the chips were of the low-fat variety. The bad news is that I ate half a bag.

Wait. It gets worse.

Then, a couple hours ago I found myself in the drive-through lane at McDonald's. But it TOTALLY wasn't my fault. After forgetting to pack a lunch for my teenager, I promised to deliver a sandwich to her school office. When I realized I didn't have any bread in the house, I found myself forced to drive through McDonald's and purchase a cheeseburger and fries for her. And, as you can well imagine, the only way to keep myself from eating her french fries while I drove was to buy a second burger and fries of my very own.

The next thing I know I'm driving down the highway and smelling french fries and salivating at the thought of chasing down my breakfast of cookies and chips with a nice, greasy burger when suddenly I think to myself:

LINAMEN, GET A GRIP!

Sure, I started a diet on January 1 just like you did. But here I am, already two weeks strong into a hearty binge.

Say it ain't so.

You know, starting a diet is one thing. Starting it for the eighty-seventh time gets a little tedious.

Anyway, I was thinking about all this while driving down the freeway when suddenly I got the strong urge to take charge of my life and climb back on the rabbit food wagon, forsaking greasy pleasures for celery and salads. I almost chucked my cheeseburger out the window until I realized that the only thing worse than starting a diet for the eighty-seventh time would be starting a diet for the eighty-seventh time AND having to pay a $200 littering fine to boot.

A few minutes later I walked into Kaitlyn's school office carrying two sacks. I dropped one sack on Mrs. Crumpton's desk and waved the other. "Does anyone want a burger and fries?"

Mrs. Stracener said, "Did they give you an extra one?"

"Nope. It's mine." And then I blurted the whole ugly story, about the chips and the cookies and the two-week binge and realizing I needed to GET A GRIP and feeling desperate and nearly getting fined for littering—

About that time Mrs. Crumpton grabbed my hands, looked solidly into my eyes, and said reassuringly, "We can help you, dear."

"Thank you!" I gushed. "Just don't let me eat the fries . . . whatever you do, DON'T LET ME EAT THE FRIES!"

So now I'm back on my diet, and there are two women in Texas who think what I really should be on is medication.

I hate starting over. It doesn't matter if the thing I'm starting over is a diet or a page of prose that I should have had saved when my dog tripped over the electrical cord to my computer.

The other thing I hate to do is start over when I stumble in my walk with Jesus. Somehow, I'd love to deal with a sin or doubt or fear or struggle once and never have to deal with it again. I'd love to announce—when the topic of gossip or lust or envy comes up—"Been there, done that!"

I'd love to say, "Anger? Oh sure. I got angry back in 1974, but the Lord delivered me, and I've been gracious ever since."

"Depression? Did that in '87. Never struggled since."

"Lack of faith? Lord and I put that one to bed back in '93."

The good news is that even when I'm feeling defeated from having to muster a brand-new attack on a not-so-new enemy, there's Someone standing by with fresh resources to see me through. Indeed, the Bible promises us that God's mercies and compassion never fail. In fact, they are new every morning, and his faithfulness is great!

Even when I'm weak, he is strong.

Which is reassuring. Especially since I only ate half the bag of chips this morning. I think the other half is still waiting for me in the kitchen.

17

Battle Strategies for Lovers

WE'VE ALL HEARD THE SAYING "MAKE LOVE, NOT WAR."
This is absurd. If you want my opinion, I say, "Why choose? Do both!"

After all, fighting is an unavoidable aspect of marriage. I mean, you can't share a bathroom sink or a checkbook with someone without coming close to blows from time to time.

So I figure the best marriage has to include room for making love AND war. You just have to know how to get from point A to point B, from all that blaming and fuming to a little passion and foreplay.

And if you happen to know how to do that, please e-mail me and let me know, because I haven't got a clue.

Actually, I've tried various approaches through the years, and I'll be happy to tell you what doesn't work.

Sugar cookies, for example, don't work.

I know this because Larry and I had a fight last week. As we were arguing, I walked into the kitchen, removed a tub of cookie dough from the freezer, and dropped a dozen chunks of dough onto a baking stone without letting my side of the debate lag for even a moment.

Twelve minutes later I grabbed a spatula, slid the perfectly browned cookies onto a plate, then poured one glass of milk.

About that time Larry commented on my Betty Crocker response to marital discord. He said, "What are you doing?"

"I'm going to eat this entire plate of cookies."

"Don't I get some?"

"I hadn't planned on it."

We didn't end up in bed. Hard to believe, isn't it?

So bingeing on sugar cookies isn't the answer. Especially if you're not willing to share.

The other thing that fails to move a hostile couple from griping to groping would be acts of violence against helpless household appliances. I learned this one evening when I threw Larry's alarm clock out of a second-story window. Trust me when I say this did not prompt him to stop waving the credit card bill in the air and take me in his arms.

Go figure.

I did feel bad about that one, though. I decided to apologize by giving him a new alarm clock along with a note that said, "I guess having fun isn't the only way to make time fly!"

Unfortunately, I never got to write the funny note. Larry was able to repair his old clock, so I had to settle on apologizing in a run-of-the-mill fashion unenhanced by my sparkling wit.

And then we kissed and made up.

Darn. You know what that means, don't you?

It means I just stumbled upon one way to get from point A to point B—from being rivals to being lovers—and it has to do with mastering the knack of apologizing.

Which is a bummer, because I'd much rather eat sugar cookies than my words.

But there it is, a hard-to-swallow fact of life: An apology works wonders at restoring harmony and romance in a marriage.

Actually, knowing how to apologize when we've made a mistake not only keeps our marriages vibrant but keeps our relationship with God healthy as well. Read Mathew 5:23 and 24. Now, I'm not a Bible scholar, but here's what I get from those verses: The next time I'm in church making an offering to God of anything—my time, dollars, or praise—and I suddenly remember that I've wronged someone, I should leave the building, get in my car, drive to that person's house, patch things up, and then get back to church and finish my business with God. Unless, of course, the person is standing next to me. In that case I suppose I could skip the driving part. But you get the idea.

And if I'm the person who was wronged and stayed miffed, the Bible's just as clear. Mark 11:25 tells me that the next time I'm praying, if I'm holding a grudge against anyone, I'd better 'fess up and forgive or else all that unforgiveness in me will hinder God from being able to forgive all the stuff I've done wrong.

Tough stuff. Easier said than done.

But maybe, in the end, keeping our relationships—with each other and with God—free and clear of the debris of grudges is actually the easier way to live. It's certainly more fun.

And if the person with whom you need to degrudgulate happens to be your husband, well, it's possible that all that kissing and making up just might work up an appetite. If so, you could always end up in the kitchen for a little post-reconciliatory snack.

Sugar cookies always work for me.

18

Read My Lips

I SAW THIS GREAT BUMPER STICKER YESTERDAY.
It said, "Oh, Evolve."

I saw another bumper sticker a couple weeks ago. It wasn't nearly as subtle. It said, "Men Are Idiots And I Married Their King."

What was particularly funny is that the King was driving the car.

We love to make statements, don't we? On our bumpers, our T-shirts . . .

And speaking of clothing statements, the one I've never quite understood is the whole deal with B.U.M. Equipment. Why a man would wear a shirt announcing that to the entire world is beyond me.

And don't even get me started on jewelry. I know that kids these days are trying to make a statement with the whole body piercing thing. I've seen some of the places people are getting pierced, though, and the only thing they seem to be saying is, "I never should have had that last drink."

The truth is, personal statements fascinate me, whether we're talking about someone using their car, clothing, or their web site to say, "This is who I am, and here's what I think about this or that."

And what about statements of faith? I don't know about your household, but there are more WWJD bracelets floating around mine than wrists to wear them. And plenty of T-shirts sporting Bible verses or faith-inspired phrases.

Here's the thing with wearing your faith on your sleeve, so to speak. It helps if you put your actions where your mouth is. It's like the time about ten years ago I was driving down the road and pulled in behind a sedan sporting the bumper sticker that said, "Honk If You Love Jesus!" (Remember those?) So I honked. Now, it's possible the man driving the sedan thought I was trying to hurry him along. In any case, he indicated his displeasure by twisting around in his seat and flashing me a lone finger (and it wasn't the "One Way" sign either!).

I'm all for catchy slogans. "Honk if you love Jesus" was catchy. "Smile, Jesus loves you" was catchy. Even WWJD was catchy.

I've got one that's not so catchy, but I'd love to see it catch on nonetheless. But, as illustrated by our finger-waving friend in the sedan, it's got to be accompanied by the right actions to carry any punch.

It goes like this:

HCILJLYTM?

Now, THERE'S a great statement. I realize it's about as pronounceable as the name of The Artist Formerly Known As Prince, but it's a great statement nonetheless. In fact, I'd love to launch a national campaign with this statement. I'd love to print it on billboards and bumper stickers and T-shirts. (Okay, so they'd have to be size XL to handle all the letters, but still . . .)

HCILJLYTM?

It could revolutionize your world.

The meaning? Simple: How Can I Let Jesus Love You Through Me?

Okay, so I don't have the shirts printed yet, the bumper stickers are still in the art department, and we had to go back to the drawing board with the earrings (too heavy; potential spinal column compression).

But even if you don't have the paraphernalia, wear the attitude. Be an instrument of God's love in the lives of those around you. Offer an encouraging word, a helping hand, a sacrificial gift. Better yet, take the guesswork out of it. Go up to your husband or your kids or your mom or your best friend or your pastor and ask outright: "How can I let Jesus love you through me today?"

And then do it.

In fact, I would really love to hear your stories. E-mail me at thefunnyfarm@email.com and let me know what happens.

And in the meantime, I'll keep working on those T-shirts.

Watch for them this spring in the plus size department of your local Christian bookstore.

19

Who Loves Ya, Baby?

I EAVESDROPPED ON MY FIVE-YEAR-OLD the other night. She was all tucked into bed, waiting for me to come in and tell her a story, when she decided to sing herself a song.

I was in the hallway, approaching her bedroom door, when I heard the familiar words in her child's voice:

"Jesus loves me, this I know, for the Bible tells me so."

I stopped in my tracks and listened, feelings of joy and gratitude welling up inside of me. This is because nothing blesses a mother's heart like witnessing her children engaging in true worship. I knew I was on hallowed ground as I observed a precious moment in my little one's relationship with her Creator.

Kacie sang for several minutes. Then she paused, regrouped, and began again. This time there was a slight alteration in the words.

She exchanged "Jesus" for "Walter."

As in, "Walter loves me, this I know."

Walter is our German shepherd.

Okay, so it was still a nice moment, although I have to admit it left me with a few questions about Kacie's theology. One day soon, remind me to have a talk with Kacie about how God is different from a German shepherd.

Although, really, when you think about it, I guess I can't blame her. I mean, fully grasping what it means to be loved by Someone you can't see or touch is a pretty tough concept for a five year old.

It can be a tough concept to grasp even when you're forty.

Let's face it. When Walter loves you, you KNOW it. This is because even though Walter is only 7 months old and merely half of his adult weight, he has no shortage of energy and mass. At fifty pounds, he has a tendency to gallop through the house like a Shetland pony on Metabolife.

And when Walter's feeling affectionate, watch out: He slobbers. He jumps and skids around on the kitchen linoleum. He flings his body, not unlike a heat-seeking missile, at any warm-blooded target in the room. He wags his tail so hard he's been known to send furniture and compact vehicles flying. In short, his affection is so tangible that it can put you in the hospital if you're not careful.

Then there's God, who is invisible and intangible and does not dispense bruises, saliva, or dog hair.

Have you ever wished God were a bit more tangible?

I have.

Ever wished you could see his face, hear his audible voice, feel his arms around you?

Me too.

In fact, I was feeling that way just last Sunday. Had a bad week and was apparently wearing it on my face, because friend Kathy Clegg came up to me and said, "How are you doing?"

And I could tell she really wanted to know.

"Not good," I said.

"I know. I can tell. You look like you need a hug." And she hugged me.

The truth is, I've had some struggles in my life the past couple years, and I've been blessed to have some really wonderful friends rally around me. They don't always agree with me, or condone everything I think or say or do, but they've been loving me nonetheless with their smiles and their words and their hugs.

And in the process, well, a sort of magic has been occurring as the invisible, intangible God has been showing up in my life in a visible, tangible manner.

How do I know this is happening?

For starters, he just *feels* closer, which is nice—I certainly won't knock it—but the real proof is in the pudding, as it's written in 1 John 4:11–12. These verses say, basically, "Dear ones, if God loved us THIS much—enough to send his Son Jesus into the world to pay the price for our wrongdoings—then we should love each other. It's true that no one has ever seen God, but if we love each other, God dwells in us."

If we love each other, the Invisible dwells in us. God shows up. He's there. He's present. On top of all that, his love isn't intangible at all, not when it's being lived out through flesh-and-blood friends who are ready and willing to dispense hugs, helping hands, chicken soup, carpool favors, greeting cards, good advice, and even a shoulder to cry on.

You want a tangible God? Then get vulnerable with huggable friends who have Jesus living in their hearts. Best yet, you won't have to brush dog hairs off your clothes when you're done.

20

Dahling, You Look Marvelous!

A COUPLE SUNDAYS AGO I WAS APPROACHED BY A WOMAN in the church foyer. She said, "You've lost more weight! You're looking so good! I can really tell a difference. You look really great."

Just about the time my head was approaching a circumference that would have hindered me from walking through the double doors into the church sanctuary, she reached up and began to fuss with a lock of my hair.

"Now you just need to update your hair. One of those cute new 'dos. Yes, that would do wonders. That's definitely what you need!"

I thanked her and moved on.

What else could I have done? Perhaps I should have said, "I couldn't agree with you more, Mary! In fact, I'll get that new hairdo as soon as you get that brow lift you've been talking about. They're doing wonderful things with lasers these days! You shouldn't hesitate another minute!"

No, no, that wouldn't have done at all.

Now I'll be the first to admit that sometimes it's hard to know what to say and what not to say. After all, there are certain sensitive issues I desperately WANT my friends to discuss with me.

For example, after lunch one day last week I dropped by the church office to give a bulletin insert to Monique, our church secretary. Associate Pastor Scott and Senior Pastor Toby were in the office as well, and the four of us soon found ourselves engaged in a lively conversation. (If I remember right, Toby was telling us about the time he dressed in women's clothing for a youth fundraiser. He said the stockings were bearable, but that there should be laws banning the use of eyelash curlers by the untrained).

After the men left the office, I looked down and noticed a large piece of lettuce resting on my left breast.

"Monique!" I squealed. "Why didn't you tell me I'm modeling my lunch on my mammary glands!"

She winced. "I tried to signal you, but you didn't see me. I couldn't very well have interrupted the pastor's story to say, 'Karen, taco salad alert, left nipple.'"

She was right, of course. But in general, I'm grateful when my friends alert me to lipstick on my teeth or spinach at my gumline.

So here are the rules: It's okay to comment on C-cup lettuce leaves, but diss my hairstyle and die.

You can see why it gets a little confusing at times . . . why it's easy to mess up and say the wrong thing at the wrong time . . . why you and I both have been on the receiving end (and the giving end) of the kind of comments that have the power to produce a shudder or a wince.

Ever let a friendship drift because someone said something to you—something that may have been thoughtless or perhaps even encouragement-gone-awry but certainly was never intended to offend—and you just couldn't get over it?

Guys don't have this problem. I don't know why. They say things to each other all the time that would send a woman into therapy. My dad used to greet one of his best friends regularly with the phrase, "Hey, Uglier-Than-Me!" And his friend just laughed. Can you imagine saying that to one of your girlfriends? At best, she would never speak to you again. At worst, you'd have to call me some afternoon to pick you up from the mall after you returned to the parking lot and found your tires slashed.

Or maybe those kinds of comments bother guys, but guys are just better at letting them go. My husband holds a grudge for about the length of a television commercial. My grudges, on the other hand, tend to become elevated to the status of distinguished family members. I give them names, chart their growth, and celebrate their birthdays.

Remember the television ad from many moons ago? The one in which we were reminded that "A mind is a terrible thing to waste"?

Well, so is a friendship.

If you have a friend who is always putting you down with her comments, you might want to ask her why or work on establishing healthier boundaries in your relationship.

But if you find yourself smarting from an unfortunate comment in a usually loving friendship, I have three words for you: Get over it.

Mention it if you need to, work it out, reaffirm your friendship, then get over it and go on.

You know, the Lord didn't mess up. He's placed you and me smack dab in the middle of chaotic relationships with imperfect people because the bumpy road of loving and being loved leaves us richer as a result.

Margery Williams gets credited with coming up with the Velveteen Rabbit Principle. And yet our heavenly Father has had a handle on this principle for eons. He knows that in the process of loving and being loved, we're going to get bumped and bruised now and then. We're going to fray at the edges and get dropped in the mud and even spend some nights forgotten and abandoned in the cold. We may even end up sporting a few scars, because sometimes love hurts.

But when it's all said and done, relationships—even chaotic relationships with imperfect people—leave us richer than before. They shape our souls. They make us real.

They may even make us better looking.

I'd explain more but I don't have time. I've got to grab my purse and hurry out the door.

Supercuts closes in half an hour.

21

Wanna Enrich Your Life?
Swap Insights
with Your Friends

I'M ALWAYS TRYING TO TALK MY FRIENDS INTO THINGS.

Take this week for example. I've tried to talk a half dozen women into taking this class with me. It's an eight-week class and it's very reasonably priced and we'd be having fun and getting great exercise as well. What more could you ask for?

I just don't understand why I'm not getting any takers. I thought EVERYBODY harbored a secret wish to take belly-dancing lessons. I just don't get the reticence.

Maybe it's the Armenian blood in me. Either that or I spent too many hours as a kid watching *I Dream of Jeannie.*

No, wait, I bet I know what influenced me. No doubt it was that awesome photo of Liz Curtis Higgs in a veil and two pounds of eyeliner on the cover of her excellent book *Bad Girls of the Bible.* (There's no way you can convince me there's not a navel ring hiding beneath all those layers of silk!) Be that as it may, so far my friends don't share my enthusiasm about the lessons. But I'll be sure to keep you informed.

The point is, my friends and I are always swapping ideas on how to make our lives more interesting or productive or healthy. Okay, so I'll admit the bellydancing brainstorm might have been a little over the top. Normally our ideas are much more mainstream.

Like the way we're always swapping diet strategies and newsflashes. Last week, for example, I got a phone call from a friend of mine. She sounded positively manic as she squealed, "You'll never guess what happened last night!"

I wondered if she had won the lottery. I was getting ready to ask her to pay for my bellydancing lessons when she said, "I got into my blue jeans!"

She hasn't worn blue jeans in a year. But after dieting and exercising for several weeks, she got those denims zipped.

I understand the significance of her news. I've fought the battle of the bulge myself. The truth is, winning the lottery pales in comparison to getting back into a favorite pair of jeans after a cellulite-induced exile.

We also encourage each other when it comes to beauty secrets.

And, boy, do we need those beauty secrets. Can anyone explain to me why, as we get older, our eyebrows, lips, hair and bones get thinner while our waistlines continue to thicken? It hardly seems fair.

Not to mention what happens to our eyelids. Last week my friend Beth lamented, "It's getting harder to put on eyeliner. My eyelids are too wrinkly."

I know what she's talking about. It's not easy getting liner up and down both sides of all those tiny wrinkles.

Half the time my eyelids sport a dotted line.

I have good news on the hair removal front, though. Several chapters ago I confessed that I had an appointment for electrolysis to remove a dozen stubborn chin hairs. I've had more than one reader write and ask me how it went. Here's the report: I love the results! You'll be glad to know that my chin stubble days are behind me. I no longer look like Michael W. Smith, which is thrilling to me although my fourteen-year-old daughter says she misses snickering at my rendition of "Rocketown."

Electrolysis tip: Take a Walkman and listen to your favorite music as your hair follicles are getting zapped. And turn the beat up loud—with enough decibels it's possible to drown out some of the pain. (But not too loud. Your electrologist will be determining the voltage via a foot pedal. You do NOT want her tapping her toes to the beat. Trust me on this.)

And when my friends and I aren't trading health and beauty secrets, we can often be found talking about the relationships in our lives. We ask each other questions like these . . .

How can I teach my kids to be more respectful? How can I forgive my husband? How can I encourage a friend who's going through a tough time? I'm lonely—how can I create more meaningful bonds with people around me? How can I get rid of the anger I feel toward my ex? How can I get my kids to be more responsible? Do I criticize my husband too much? If so, how can I build him up instead? How can I set boundaries at work? How can I get along better with my parents?

From there the categories get even broader. The Bible says God forgives me for my past mistakes—why can't I seem to forgive myself? How can I stay consistent in God's Word? Why do I have a hard time believing that Jesus loves me? How can I experience more power in my prayer life? I'm struggling with lust or envy or bitterness—any suggestions how I can win this battle? How can I get a handle on my depression? I can't seem to trust God about my situation—how can I learn to trust him more?

I love having these kinds of conversations with my friends. And if you're not broaching these kinds of topics with godly girlfriends in your life, maybe you should give it a try.

I find that my friends are a wealth of practical information. No one friend has all the answers, but between them all I've gathered useful insights on everything from fixing my cat to fixing my marriage, from bleaching my teeth to harnessing my tongue, from balancing my checkbook to balancing my life.

And what's really great is that you and I can have these kinds of intimate, encouraging conversations with our friends any time, anywhere. We don't have to make a formal appointment! We can encourage each other over coffee at our kitchen tables, via cell phones as we commute home from work, or side by side as we browse garage sales or watch our kids play softball.

In fact, I was sort of hoping Thursday nights would provide an opportunity for these kinds of conversations with my friends as we drove to our bellydancing classes.

If that sounds like fun to you, give me a call.

As of this moment, there's still plenty of room in the car.

22

Never Underestimate the Power of an Imperfect Woman

I REMEMBER THE DAY KACIE, THEN FOUR, WALKED into my office and announced, "I'm ready to go to the party."

Indeed, Kacie was supposed to attend a birthday party in a couple hours. I looked at her. She was wearing her Princess Barbie nightgown.

"Kacie, you can't wear that to a birthday party. That's a nightgown."

"Mom, it's a nightgown at NIGHT. Today it's a dress. I'm wearing this to the party."

Immediately I thought back to my childhood. When I was growing up, there were rules about these sort of things. People understood the meaning of the word etiquette. We not only didn't wear pajamas to birthday parties, we didn't even wear our play clothes. We wore party dresses, for crying out loud. We had standards. We had manners. This is what made America great.

All this was running through my head as I evaluated Kacie's request.

"This is what I want to wear," Kacie repeated.

"All right," I said. "But the Winnie the Pooh slippers have got to go."

I've got SOME standards, after all.

In my defense let me remind you that I'm forty, not to mention the fact that Kacie is my second child. We forty-year-old women simply do not have the energy to raise our second, third, or fourth children as diligently as we raised our first-borns back when big hair and leggings were in style.

So Kacie wore the Princess Barbie nightgown. I did, however, take extra pains adorning her hair with pink ribbons, and I made her wear frilly socks and Sunday shoes.

After all, I didn't want the other women to think of my daughter as a poor, neglected child whose mother would pack her off to a party in pajamas.

No way. I wanted them to realize this was a beloved and well-cared-for child whose mother would pack her off to a party in pajamas.

There IS a difference.

Look, I came to grips several years ago with the fact that I'm not Superwoman.

That was always my dream. I wanted to be Superwoman. When it came to homemaking, marriage, being a friend, and especially raising my kids, I wanted "perfection" to be my middle name.

Unfortunately, I soon discovered that I'm hard-pressed to outrun a speeding toddler much less a speeding bullet. And leaping tall buildings in a single bound isn't even in the realm of reality—not after I sprained my ankle trying to hop over a sprawling Barbie metropolis my kids erected in my kitchen one rainy afternoon.

So I'm not Superwoman.

How can I be so sure?

Not only would a real Superwoman refrain from sending her child to a birthday party in Barbie pajamas, she also would never be rushing to get ready for an important job interview, nick her leg shaving, and have to walk out the door wearing a Muppet Babies Band-Aid under her hose.

Furthermore, a real Superwoman would never hang up on her editor while shouting the phrase, "I have to go! The baby's in the toilet!", and she CERTAINLY would not be growing eleven different strains of penicillin in her refrigerator.

I used to want people to think I was perfect.

Now I'm relieved when they realize I'm not.

Frequently folks write reviews of my books, and one review in particular made me want to hug the writer when she referred to my tendency to use the smoke alarm interchangeably with the oven timer and then went on to observe: "This woman is a nonthreatening teacher. We are convinced that she needs help, but since we do too, we will accept any pearls she has to offer."

Have you ever looked at your life and thought, "I'd love to be a positive influence in someone's life, but my own life feels too flawed/chaotic/imperfect/unorganized/broken for me to have anything worthwhile to offer"?

Yeah, me too.

But I'm wondering if you and I don't have it all backwards. Maybe our struggles and imperfections don't disqualify us from reaching out to others after all. Maybe they are, indeed, the very things that give us not just credibility, but compassion as well.

For example, I have a couple friends who have experienced depression, as I have. When I feel myself slipping back into the abyss that claimed my life for several years, these are the women I turn to. Do they have all the answers? No way. Sometimes they still struggle too!

But the real reason I turn to these friends isn't for their solutions. It's for the passion I see in their faces when they look me in the eyes and say, "I know you're tired. But please hang on. You can get through this."

The truth is, accountability and encouragement coming from someone who appears to have her own life completely "together" can feel stifling and obtrusive.

But accountability and encouragement coming from a friend who has scars and wounds of her own is both humbling and empowering.

Am I Superwoman? No way.

Are you Superwoman? I don't think I'm going out on a limb here by saying "Fat chance."

Isn't that great? That means you and I have the credentials to encourage, inspire, entertain, educate, mentor, train, teach, laugh with, walk with, and cry with each other all the way through this crazy ride called life.

Which means we can relax. In fact, wouldn't it be great to get together some evening, maybe at a favorite restaurant, and linger over coffee and pie as we laugh and talk? We could leave our façades at home and talk about our shortcomings, and how God manages to use us to bless others in spite of ourselves, and how he uses other imperfect folks to bless us.

In fact, you pick the restaurant and I'll meet you there. You shouldn't have any trouble recognizing me.

I'll be the one in my pajamas.

23

The Sunday Morning Comics (and other Indispensable Gardening Tools)

TWO DAYS AGO A WOMAN SAID TO ME, "I'd love to see your garden sometime."

Sara has never been to my home, but she read about my gardening efforts in my book *Just Hand Over the Chocolate and No One Will Get Hurt.*

In the book I painted vivid pictures of daylilies and holly-hocks, morning glories and hydrangeas. I described hours spent puttering in the dirt with my kids, playing with cater-pillars and watering cans.

I smiled lamely at Sara. "Oh," I said. "The Garden."

My garden was once as beautiful as I described. But if Sara came to my house today she would find one neglected bed of pansies, an overgrown trellis of Lady Banksia roses, and some diehard lamb's ears.

Not to mention weeds.

You see, last summer I was feeling sort of overwhelmed and found myself trying to simplify my life. It was while in this state of mind that I thought about the amount of water it was going to take to keep my garden thriving through the scorching Texas summer. Somehow, I came to the conclusion I could save time and money by letting my garden succumb to the heat and simply purchasing all new plants in the spring.

So now it's April, and I'm thinking I should just go down to the bank and take out a second mortgage on my home. Or add Home Depot to the signature card on my checking account. Or sell my children to the gypsies. After all, replenishing all my beds with blooms isn't going to go easy on my wallet. In fact, I suspect the National Debt will seem quite manageable in comparison.

Not to mention the labor it's going to require.

But when it comes to reclaiming the yard, at least I got a good start yesterday: I made my fourteen-year-old mow the lawn.

Those of you with teenagers realize this is no small accomplishment. I figure I could have reseeded the lawn, put in a vegetable garden, and built a wooden deck with the amount of energy it took to prod, threaten, and cajole my teen into finishing the task at hand. Which begs the question: Why is it that a teen who can't hear a mother's instructions at three paces can hear the ring of the kitchen phone twenty yards away over the drone of one lawnmower and a headset blaring "Collide" by Jars of Clay?

Of course, my teen is easier to motivate when the riding mower is working (I think she pretends it's an SUV). But ever since the riding mower conked out and she's been stuck with the gas-powered push model, getting an hour's labor out of her requires nothing short of a cattle prod and an act of Congress.

But the gardening device I'm really anxious to try is my mini-tiller. I bought it last fall and have yet to break ground with it. According to the glowing advertising claims that prompted me to part with an amount of money that could have fed and clothed a third-world country for the better part of a year, this machine not only tills, weeds, aerates, mulches, trims, and edges, it should give me thinner thighs and whiter teeth as well.

What the company neglected to tell me was that my 400-horsepower weed-busting Garden Genie would be delivered to me, ready-to-be-assembled, in a shoebox.

I've seen head lice larger than the hundreds of parts I'm supposed to be able to assemble into a gasoline-driven work-horse in only 1,047 easy steps.

Which is why the Garden Genie is still in its shoebox, and last week my daughters and I prepared our first flower bed of the season by throwing layers of newspaper down on the weeds and then covering them up with four bags of potting soil. (The downside is that I'll have to plant flowers with very shallow root systems, at least until the newspaper finishes killing the weeds and then decomposes. In hindsight, taking the potting soil out of the plastic bags might not have been a bad idea either.)

You know, gardening can be enjoyable labor.

Or it can feel frustrating and even futile.

A lot depends on whether or not you've got the right tools.

Resources like the right mower, a handy tiller, and adequate water can make a world of difference when you're in the process of nurturing tender growing things.

Cultivating soil with a weedwacker, for example, is a recipe for disaster. Cutting grass with cuticle scissors is a one-way ticket to the Funny Farm. And planting bulbs with a kitchen spoon not only takes twice as long but can make your coffee taste kind of earthy the next morning.

I understand these principles when it comes to organic growth (just don't ask me how I knew about the earthy coffee).

So why do I forget they apply to spiritual growth as well?

I want to grow, thrive, bloom, and bear fruit spiritually. But am I equipping myself with the right tools? Or am I trying to do the job armed with a teaspoon and the Sunday funnies?

What are the power tools of spiritual growth? This list isn't definitive, but I've got a few ideas: Prayer. Fasting. The Word of God. Praise and worship. Accountability to godly friends. Confession. Bible study. Spending time in the presence of God.

I don't know about you, but some days I think my backyard is a tropical paradise compared to my spiritual landscaping.

Spring is a great time to spruce up the yard. But maybe it's a good reminder to tend to my soul as well.

I was going to spend the afternoon potting a few patio plants. But before I head outdoors, I think I'll spend an hour in my favorite armchair with my Bible and a cup of coffee. It should be a rewarding time.

Even if my coffee does taste like dirt.

24

Easy Does It

I GOT A MAMMOGRAM YESTERDAY.
I really liked the technician who conducted the procedure. She was a petite woman with artificial red hair, kind eyes, a smoker's voice, and a penchant for the truth.

None of this "this won't hurt a bit" stuff from this woman.

As she maneuvered me into position on the slab, she said, "Now this top thing here is going to come down hard and smoosh you flat. It'll hurt, but I'll be as quick as I can."

Yeah, it was uncomfortable, but not unbearable, which is kinda surprising considering that for about forty-five seconds my left breast was thinner than two-ply toilet paper and boasted a surface area roughly equivalent to a football field.

But I'm glad I went. I walked out of that clinic feeling really great. For one thing, certain body parts that are normally pretty sedate were no longer being forced to perform acts of contortion that seem more fitting to a troupe of circus gymnasts. I also felt great because I'd done something good for myself, although I think I had yet to bounce back to my original shape because my bra was fitting kind of funny, sort of like trying to fit a pair of cereal bowls around two Frisbees.

I was also feeling great because the doctor had said all my X rays looked normal. Not that I'd been worried or anything. In fact, when I first discovered the lump, I was so nonworried that I apparently felt the need to prove it to myself by waiting a full three months to schedule my mammogram. Of course, I didn't REALIZE I was trying to prove something to myself. I THOUGHT I was merely busy. After awhile, however, I began to suspect that I wasn't rushing to make my appointment because I was attempting to act nonchalant about something that, theoretically, didn't concern me a bit. It wasn't until the day of my test that I admitted to myself the reason I was trying so hard to be nonchalant was because I was really pretty scared.

I don't want to do that again. By "that" I mean turn something simple (get a mammogram and get it now) into something all complicated and embellished with dark thoughts and borrowed fears.

I think, when it comes to mammograms, I need to remember to K.I.S.S.—"Keep It Simple, Stupid."

In fact, now that I'm forty and am supposed to get a routine mammogram once a year, I think I'll schedule it each April and start thinking of it as my annual birthday present to myself.

Here's another thought: What if we women turned mammograms into a Girlfriend Event, kind of like going shopping or getting our nails done together. We could call each other on the phone and say, "Let's do something fun together this week. I know—let's get mammograms!"

No mind games. No flirting with denial. No putting it off because we're preoccupied with crossing scary bridges before we come to them. Just taking something good for us and reframing it as a present we give ourselves. Simple.

There's something else I'd like to simplify in my life, and it has to do with . . .

. . . chocolate.

I've decided that the next time you or I have an insatiable craving for chocolate, we should make things simple and just GO FOR IT. In fact, we shouldn't hesitate a minute! This is because, by my calculations, we will actually SAVE CALORIES if we immediately locate some chocolate and consume it with relish (passionate relish, not pickle relish, which may go well with hot dogs but can really take the enjoyment out of a Hershey's).

I say that eating chocolate at the first sign of an insatiable craving will actually help you save calories because it will help you avoid the following scenario.

One day, in the throes of an insatiable craving, I sat down at my computer in a panic and e-mailed something along the lines of the following sentiments to a friend:

"Help! I'm feeling stressed and overwhelmed and all I want to do is go to the freezer and eat a chocolate ice cream sandwich. So far, in order to avoid eating this ice cream sandwich, I've consumed four bananas, six bagels with lowfat cream cheese, five containers of Yoplait nonfat yogurt, nine sticks of fat-free Mozzarella cheese, and now I'm writing you in a desperate attempt to keep my hands occupied so they don't lead me to the freezer and feed me, against my will, the ice cream sandwich which is continuing to call my name even as I type."

The next morning Chris e-mailed back: "I think you should have eaten the ice cream sandwich."

Good advice. If I had eaten the ice cream sandwich and satisfied my craving, I would have actually consumed 3,475 fewer calories than I managed to consume by not eating the ice cream sandwich.

Sometimes we make things more complicated than we need to, don't we? We try so hard to manage our emotions and our lives, and sometimes, in the process, we end up complicating everything to no end.

Like the prayer thing I decided to do.

I've been seeing this really neat Christian counselor, and one day we were talking about how every morning he kneels in his living room and prays. He thinks of it as "getting online" with God, maybe like a DSL line or something that stays logged on all day. In any case, every morning he prays, "Okay Lord, here I am. I'm asking you to live today through me, because, on my own, I'm going to fall short. Be with me today, in me, living the Christian walk through me, because I can't do it any other way. Amen."

I said, "That sounds simple. I'd like to do that. In fact, I'm going to start doing it this very week."

Three weeks later I had yet to pray that prayer in the morning. I told John, "Whoops, I'd better write this down, make myself a note or a list or something, to remind myself to pray."

He said, "Don't make a list. Don't make it so complicated. A list means you're trying to force yourself to do it on your own. Making a list is religion, not a relationship. Instead, driving home today, say, 'Lord, remind me this week to talk to you every morning. I really want to do this, but left on my own, well, quite honestly, I'm probably going to forget, just like I've been forgetting for the past three weeks. But if you wouldn't mind reminding me, I'd really like to do this.'"

That made sense. It really did sound more like, well, a relationship. So I asked him to remind me. And guess what? He's been doing it. Every morning.

Am I complicating my faith by relying too much on my own religious efforts? Or can I simplify my walk with Jesus, experiencing it more as a living partnership than a list of daily do's that falls squarely on my shoulders? It's a new concept for me. I'll let you know how it continues to develop.

In fact, you can help me out. The next time I try to take something simple—like a mammogram, a chocolate craving, or even my walk with Jesus—and turn it into something convoluted and complex, just drop me a note, will you?

It can say, "Don't forget to K.I.S.S."

25

In the company of critters

KACIE LOVES CRITTERS.

In fact she loves animals of all kinds, including invisible ones.
Case in point: She's got this imaginary friend named Tito.
She began talking about Tito a couple years ago. Best we
can tell, Tito is a dog. He also has a girlfriend named Marie.

Sometimes Tito has a bit of a mean streak. Like the time I
was driving and looked into my rearview mirror and saw Kacie
sitting quietly in her car seat, tears streaming down her face.

"Kacie! What's wrong?"

She blinked. "Tito bit me."

All our friends at church know about Tito. One man in particular enjoys teasing Kacie about Tito. Practically every time
he sees Kacie, Herschel asks, "How's Tito?"

Sometimes Kacie tells him. Increasingly, however, Kacie
merely crosses her arms and purses her lips as if to say, "Oh
puh-lease, not again."

One day another friend overheard Herschel teasing Kacie. His curiosity piqued, Condall just had to ask, "Who in the world is Tito?"

Herschel told him.

Condall thought the whole thing was great and figured he'd get in on the fun. Squatting eye-level with Kacie, he grinned and said, "Hey Kacie, how's Tito?"

Kacie never even blinked. She eyeballed him back and said levelly, "Tito's dead."

So Herschel and Condall killed Tito. Tito stayed dead for several months until Marie managed to bring him back to life. Kacie explained that Marie did this with some sort of magic stones. I figured Kacie and Marie assumed this was safe to do because Herschel and Condall had finally stopped asking about Tito.

Tito may have a mean streak, but he seems to appreciate his privacy.

When Kacie's not playing with invisible friends, the other critters she loves are garden critters. She's always begging me to help her find pill bugs, June bugs, crickets, even snakes.

She really loves the snakes. Little baby garden snakes. She gets this death grip around their little bodies and hangs on tight.

I always watch her closely when she's playing with snakes. I'm not worried about her physical safety as much as her psychological health. I don't think it's healthy for a child to have to live with the fact that she inadvertently squeezed the life out of a baby snake with her bare hands.

Besides, Kacie's probably already going to need therapy, what with having to kill Tito off like that.

In any case, the other day Kacie and I were wrapping up a day spent in the garden. Kacie had just spent the afternoon with many of her favorite critters. She had collected rollie pollies, chased crickets, prodded worms, studied ants, and befriended several moths.

It had been a well-populated afternoon, although if I remember right, Tito was nowhere to be seen (which, come to think of it, is probably to be expected for an invisible dog). On our way inside for dinner, Kacie needled me with several dozen questions about worms and crickets and pill bugs and ants. I found myself explaining how all these critters and many others form a sort of community. I told her that the worms aerate the soil, and the bees pollinate the flowers, and the crickets . . . well, I don't really know what crickets do, but I'm sure I made something up and managed to sound fairly credible in the process.

I told her that each critter was important, and that our garden just wouldn't be the same without them all.

And I've been thinking about that conversation ever since.

I'm part of a community, too. I won't say if I'm more like the hardworking ant or the social butterfly (nectar, anyone?), but my point is that I am part of a community of critters, and every one of us has a unique role to fill. There are the quiet laborers, the encouragers, the movers and the shakers, the problem solvers and the huggers. In my community (as in yours, no doubt) there are even a few well-meaning pests.

What a privilege it is to have these folks in my life.

You know, the Bible encourages us not to forsake fellowship with other believers. I think it's because we really do need each other. Not a one of us can thrive isolated and on our own.

Not even Tito.

He might be a little shy around Herschel and Condall, but I hear he's sticking close to Kacie and Marie these days.

They knew right where to find those magic stones, after all.

Motherhood's Unsolved Mysteries

BEFORE I WAS A PARENT, I HAD NO CHILDREN, but I had lots of theories about parenting.

Now I have two children and no theories.

Actually, the person in my home who believes she knows the most about parenting is my fourteen-year-old daughter. Of course, she thinks she knows the most about everything under the sun. She will, no doubt, get smarter and smarter until the day she gives birth to her first child. At that point, it is virtually guaranteed that she will experience a massive knowledge deficit.

Some experts believe that this "brain drain" is, in some mysterious fashion, related to the detachment of the placenta during childbirth. Others believe it is actually triggered in the months and years following childbirth, probably as a result of a prolonged exposure to seven-foot birds and purple herbivores.

Whatever the reason, the bottom line is this:

Even though you and I grew up believing that Father (and Mother) really did know best, once we became parents ourselves we suddenly discovered the Big Secret: Moms and dads don't have a clue. We just make that stuff up about being omniscient to keep knowledgeable kids in check until they, too, become parents and experience a two-thirds drop in their IQ. Then they can be in charge.

The truth is, I've been a parent long enough to know that every morning brings with it some new challenge for which I am nominally prepared. Why can't kids come with instructions? Both of my babies came home from the hospital with one of those nasal suction devices they tried to adopt as pacifiers. Why don't doctors send babies home with something their parents can really use . . . like a how-to manual?

I am constantly amazed by the number of times my kids have left me scratching my head in confusion or wonder (and I'm not even referring to the time they put dish detergent in the shampoo bottle. That's another head-scratching story altogether).

Do I know best? Sometimes I think I don't know squat.

A few of the many topics about which I don't have a clue include the following:

How serious is it when a two-year-old has a toe fetish? When Kacie was two, several times a day she demanded to have her shoes and socks removed so she could examine her feet. Is she destined to spend her adult life wearing sandals for easy access? When she's in seventh grade and has to write an essay on "Someone I Admire," will she choose Imelda Marcos? And is podiatry a good career choice for someone with a foot fetish, or does that border on the unethical?

And that's not the only mystery.

What in the world does it mean when you are setting the table for company and find a hard glob of chewed gum under the rim of your best china? Whose gum is it? Your teenage son's? When did he last eat on the good china anyway? And if it wasn't him, could one of your previous guests have done it? Shouldn't the dishwasher have melted the gum and whisked it away when the plate was washed? And if chewed gum is indeed impervious to scalding soapy water, then how long has it been there? Was it there when you served Christmas dinner to your in-laws or when you entertained your husband's boss last month?

Where do all the missing socks go?

Why is meat loaf served at a friend's house more enticing to your kids than pizza served at home?

What do teenage girls do in the bathroom for three hours?

And what exactly does it mean when your ten-year-old loses a tooth at school, brings it home in a tiny plastic box, and then leaves it sitting for two months in a corner of your kitchen counter? When Kaitlyn was ten, my countertop was adorned with an abandoned baby molar for two months. I had to ask myself, did Kaitlyn forget it was there? Had she lost sleep at night wondering where she left her tooth and longing for her dollar from the tooth fairy? If so, why hadn't she mentioned it to me? What if she didn't think her tooth was lost? What if she knew exactly where it was? What if a visit from the tooth fairy was the last thing on her mind? What if . . . what if my baby's growing up?

From potty training dilemmas to disciplinary decisions to debates about dating, driving, and the decorative piercing of body parts, motherhood offers a smorgasbord of challenging questions that promise to stump even the wisest of moms and dads.

Maybe Robert Young had all the answers when he was raising Princess, Kitten, and Bud.

But for the rest of us, parenting is a leap of faith . . . an unending series of mysteries . . . an adventure that takes us daily to our wits' end and beyond.

Do fathers know best? Do mothers?

No way.

But there is one Father who does.

It's an amazing thing, but when we enter into a relationship with God's own Son, Jesus, we find ourselves adopted into the family of God. What we used to think of as some nebulous cosmic power suddenly becomes real to us in a way we never could have imagined. The Force becomes family. That higher power turns out to be a heavenly Father. We discover that the distant deity is more along the lines of . . . well, actually, a dad.

I may be a mom, but I don't come close to having all the answers I need in my life. I need a heavenly Father to help me make sense of it all . . . to help me meet the challenge of raising my family . . . to help me achieve my potential as a parent, spouse, and human being.

You need that kind of a Dad, too.

He's got all the answers, after all. And whatever answers he doesn't give us here on earth, I'm sure he'll be willing to provide once we get to heaven.

Just remind me, when we get there, in case it's a long time from now and I forget to ask.

I'd still love to know about that gum under my china.

27

It's the Heart That Counts

I'VE BEEN OUT OF TOWN.

I spent Mother's Day weekend speaking at the Terre Haute First Assembly of God, enjoying myself and falling in love with the wonderful folks at that church. I returned home Monday morning, pulling into my driveway at 2:00 A.M.

Four hours later, I was awakened by Kacie calling my name from her bedroom. Thinking she was having a bad dream, I hurried to her side.

She was still half asleep—in fact, her eyes were still closed—as she heard my voice and blurted, "Have you been to the kitchen table yet?"

I said no.

She tumbled out of bed with excitement. "Your presents are there! Let's go!"

"Kacie, it's six in the morning! Can't we sleep a while longer?" She flashed me a look of sheer horror. "No! Your Mother's Day presents are there! We have to go right now!"

And so we did.

That's how I ended up, at 6:15 Monday morning, ooohing and aaahhhing over refrigerator magnets, a potted ink pen with a flower glued to the top, a handmade card, a new curling iron, and an iridescent purple blow-dryer. Larry's gift to me was a Mr. Coffee Iced Tea Maker.

I loved every gift.

I told Kaitlyn the curling iron was a brilliant idea, since my travels have made sharing the same curling iron a challenge (I never mentioned the fact that I bought my own curling iron in Terre Haute this weekend).

I told Larry the iced tea maker was great (I didn't mention that this is the THIRD iced tea pot he's bought for me, and that the other two are on a shelf in the laundry room because, in order to make tea, these machines require a pitcher full of ice, and I don't have an icemaker).

It was my turn, then, to give a few gifts. While on my trip, I picked up some sand-art kits for the girls and some candy.

Kacie was particularly excited about the candy. She gripped it tightly in her hand and beamed. "I had this kind of candy once before!" she said happily. "But it was too much sugar and it made me throw up!" She paused then, her smile frozen on her face and one eyebrow raised, as the implication of her statement sank in: Maybe candy that resulted in getting intimate with a commode wasn't such a great gift after all!

Thinking back on the morning, I had to laugh. So many good intentions! But even the best intentions didn't keep us from missing the target by a few inches on several of the gifts.

Did that diminish the experience for me?

Nah, somehow it just made the morning more precious.

And I realized that the real gift—the one that really glimmered against the backdrop of beautifully wrapped curling irons and tea makers, refrigerator magnets and blow-dryers—was the enthusiasm of the givers.

The real gift was the fact that Kacie's first thought after our separation was not about what I could do for her, but about what she could give to me.

The real gift was hearing from Kaitlyn that the iridescent purple blow-dryer cost more than the noniridescent purple dryer, but that she had been glad to pay the difference because she wanted me to have the very best one.

The real gift was the sacrificial efforts of a dad who has severe allergic reactions to malls and who has been known to wrap presents in trash bags.

God must understand this principle better than anyone.

That's why he cherished quarters from widows more than big bucks from hypocrites.

Have you ever thought about giving something to God—a song solo during worship service, an hour a week teaching Sunday school, participation in a local outreach or ministry—and then didn't do it because you were afraid your efforts would be less than perfect? Because you figured someone else could do the job better? Because you were terrified of making a mistake?

Yeah, me too.

What a shame.

Because the truth is that our heavenly Father cherishes the quality of our passion over the quality of our performance. He values sincerity over perfection. And he loves the givers more than he loves the gifts.

I need to remind myself of this often. Maybe even daily. In fact, maybe I should write myself a note and tape it to my bathroom mirror. It could remind me that my Father loves my heartfelt gifts to him—not because my gifts are perfect, but because he loves me with a perfect love.

I could ponder this each morning as I brush my teeth and wash my face.

Not to mention as I curl my hair, a shiny new curling iron in each hand.

28

We're Definitely Getting older ... But Are We Getting wiser?

RECENTLY A YOUNG MAN NAMED BAYLEN SHOWED ME his two front teeth. Or, rather, DIDN'T show me his two front teeth.

Baylen just turned seven. There's a gap in his smile that means he's growing up. It also makes a neat place to stick a straw and drink Dr Pepper while his jaws are clamped shut. It also makes a neat window through which he can squeeze the tip of his tongue and gross out anyone who may be watching.

Missing teeth are a welcome milestone of maturity.

Well, they're a welcome milestone of maturity when you're seven. If you're my age and older, they can mean gum disease and an artificial bridge. But when you're seven, they're way cool.

Teenagers, on the other hand, have other rites of passage. Two days ago the teenaged daughter of one of my best friends got her tongue pierced. Among her age group, this is considered a brilliant thing to do.

She called me the next morning, a note of desperation in her voice: "I need your advice. How should I tell my mom?"

I don't know why she called me. Maybe the fact that I'm the only grown-up she knows with a belly button ring had something to do with it. (Don't ask, it's a long story. Let me just say that I'm having my midlife crisis and it was far cheaper than a Ferrari.)

So I tried to be helpful. Basically, I suggested she take this approach: "Mom, I did something you're probably not going to like, but before I tell you what it is, I want you to know that keeping your trust and having a good relationship with you is really important to me, and that if you want me to undo what I've done, I will. All I ask is that, before you decide, you give me a chance to explain why I'd like to keep it."

I reminded Rachel that these couldn't be empty words. I reminded her that her relationship with her folks SHOULD be far more valuable to her than a three-quarter-inch piece of metal in her tongue.

Rachel had the talk with her mom. Amazingly, she still has her piercing. Of course, she's temporarily living on chicken broth and ice cream and talking like Scooby Doo, but she still has the stud in her tongue.

She sees it, as do her friends, as a sign of independence. But maybe the real sign of maturity is the fact that she was, indeed, willing to remove it so as not to offend her folks. She's testing boundaries, but when push came to shove, she was willing to put relationships above personal expression.

Either that or she really pulled one over on her mom and me.

Other signs of maturity? How about the fact that when you're my age and you have a birthday, you truly cannot have your cake and eat it too. This is because, in the time it takes everyone to finish singing "Happy Birthday," the cake has sustained far too much smoke and fire damage to be edible.

Other signs? I could also mention that my body's going south—like the fact that my hair is leaving my scalp and showing up on my chin—but there's enough material on THAT subject to fill an entire book, so I think I'll save it for later.

Spiritual growth is another matter. Those milestones don't come automatically with the passing of the years. It's possible to be a Christian of forty years and still have your baby teeth, so to speak. Possible to be a believer of many decades and not have learned really basic stuff, like the fact that relationships are to be cherished. Possible to have gone to church for a lot of years, but still have the naivete of a baby Christian, without any of the wisdom that tends to accompany spiritual laugh lines, hot flashes, and age spots.

Growing older is guaranteed.

Growing spiritually is a choice.

Are we growing spiritually?

What milestones should we look for?

Let's think back to when we were new believers. Think about how often we prayed, the kinds of sermons and teaching we digested, how hungry we were to read God's Word, the temptations we were struggling against. Then think about our lives today. If we can't see a lot of progress, we may be caught in a time warp: We may be forty-year-old Christians in diapers.

Of course, spiritual growth, just like physical growth, has one prerequisite: Before you can grow, you have to be born.

If you're not growing spiritually, is it because you've yet to be birthed into the family of God? If so, this is a great time for a birthday. A spiritual birthday. Talk to a pastor or a friend who attends church and tell them you're ready for a new life with Jesus. Or e-mail me and let's talk. Either way, time's short. We're not getting any younger, you and I. No use being spiritual embryos when Jesus desires to give us a full and abundant life!

So let's grow.

Good-bye baby teeth, hello molars.

The stud in the tongue is optional.

29

C'mon In, the Water's Fine

WE'RE APPROACHING BATHING SUIT SEASON.

I'm sorry, I didn't mean to be so shockingly blunt. I should have broken the bad news gently.

But it's not like we're not thinking about it already.

I've already passed racks of bathing suits in the stores and moaned.

I've already gotten bathing suit catalogs in the mail and rolled my eyes.

But it's unavoidable. Here it's June and school's out and my kids are already begging to go to the city pool. What's worse, I'm going to have to go shopping for a new suit because the last one I bought was during the Nixon administration and it's beginning to show some wear. (The suit, not the Nixon administration.)

The good news is that there are swimsuits these days designed to hide problem areas. There are skirts to hide tummies. Vertical stripes to slenderize. Bras with water-filled cups to maximize certain assets, and spandex bottom-control panels to minimize others.

I keep waiting for a suit with long sleeves.

Or maybe some flesh-colored elastic leggings to smooth out the fat deposits above my knees.

But really, I don't know what's worse. Wearing a suit that isn't flattering but is still tolerable enough to justify the expenditure of forty to eighty bucks . . . or the trauma of trying on three dozen suits that make me look horrible just to find the one that makes me look merely dumpy and unattractive.

Actually, I've been thinking about the folks who design department store dressing rooms. Obviously these folks are men. I say this because they're under the misconception that women in department store dressing rooms really want to know what they look like.

Based on this assumption, these men equip dressing rooms with bright lights and real mirrors (as opposed to candlelight and concave mirrors that take ten pounds off a woman right from the start).

I'm not saying that the men who design dressing rooms should be deceptive. I'm not saying that they should lie to us.

In fact, as far as I'm concerned, they can post a disclaimer right there in the dressing room, that says "Objects in mirror are larger than they appear."

We won't care. We already know the truth. We'll just be grateful not to have to look at every pound of it.

The truth is, I'd love to love my body.

I'd love to feel comfortable with the skin I'm in without always comparing my shape to the computer-enhanced, airbrushed curves of supermodels who not only won the gene-pool lottery but are addicted to lettuce and have the financial resources to retain the full-time services of personal trainers with names like Chip and Biff.

Even more importantly, I'd love to feel more confident about myself, knowing that my worth as a woman doesn't rise and fall with the numbers on my scale . . . that it's not diminished because of the circumference of my thighs . . . that it's not tarnished by a blemish or an age spot, knobby knees, or pear-shaped hips.

In fact, wouldn't it be great if I could draw strength and confidence and self-worth from something rock solid? Something finished and complete? Something that doesn't change from day to day? Something that—unlike my body—will never lose its vitality or bloom?

Something like that really exists. Except it's not a something. It's a Someone. And his name is Jesus. Indeed, according to the Bible . . .

. . . Jesus is the Eternal Rock.

. . . He's the Alpha and Omega, the First and the Last, the Author and Finisher of our faith.

. . . He's the same yesterday, today, and forever.

. . . And he's the Living Vine—he'll never fade or wilt or die.

Best yet, he loves me with an everlasting love.

I think I'm ready to go buy that swimsuit now. And as I look into the dressing-room mirror, I'll just remind myself that I'm loved with a love that is rock solid, complete, eternal, and alive. And if that's not enough to make me feel good about myself, I don't know what is.

Not even a bust-enhancing water-bra comes close.

30

Dogs, Teenagers, and other Noncompliant Life-forms

MY FRIEND BETH HAS A CHIHUAHUA NAMED ANNABEL.

Beth adores Annabel.

She says its because Annabel is the only member of her family who actually does what she says. And it's true. Beth says "sit" and Annabel sits. Beth says "stay" and Annabel stays.

I have a dog, too. He's a white German shepherd named Walter. I don't want to brag or anything, but Walter is just as obedient as Annabel. Honest. I give commands, and Walter obeys. It's amazing.

I say "slobber" and Walter slobbers.

I say "track mud into the house" and Walter tracks mud into the house.

I say "take the wicker loveseat on the back porch and turn it into a jumbo doggie chew toy" and Walter is only too happy to comply.

Beth and I just wish our children were as compliant as our dogs.

The thing I hate most is when I tell my kids to do something and then they stand there and argue with me.

One day I'd had it up to HERE with arguments spouting from my fourteen-year-old. I finally put my foot down. Shaking my finger at my daughter, I sputtered, "If I hear one more word from you, I'm going to put you on talking restriction!"

Beth was visiting at the time. She was sitting at my kitchen table as I issued my ultimatum. As soon as Kaitlyn left the room, Beth broke into a broad grin and said, "Now THAT made a lot of sense. Seems to me that if Kaitlyn's not allowed to say another word, she's already on talking restriction!"

Beth had a point.

Luckily, Kaitlyn never noticed the flaw in my reasoning.

Actually, she probably noticed but didn't say anything because she's so accustomed to my wacky line of thinking. The truth is, I use flawed reasoning to manage my children on a regular basis.

Like at bedtime.

Kaitlyn has always been a great negotiator. She also hates to go to bed. When she was four years old, I developed the technique of bedtime bargaining. My initial offer typically went like this:

"I'll tell you what, Kaitlyn. I want you to lay in bed real quiet, with your eyes closed, and pretend to be asleep for six hours. You don't actually have to go to sleep, all you have to do is pretend. If, after six hours, you're still awake, I'll let you get up and play the rest of the night."

Her eyes would get round as saucers. "Just six hours?"

"Just six hours."

"Six hours is too long. How about one?"

"Four."

"Two?"

I would give in with a sigh. "Oh, all right. Two hours. But not a minute less!"

Beaming victoriously, she would close her eyes and quit wiggling and lay completely still. She'd be asleep within minutes. Of course, now that Kaitlyn's fourteen, I have to resort to new techniques to get her to obey. Let me tell you about my latest strategy. It all started when I asked Kaitlyn to take a pair of shoes upstairs, and she responded by telling me all the reasons she should be allowed to leave the shoes in the stairwell until she went upstairs later in the day.

I said I didn't want the shoes in the stairwell for half the day. She still argued.

I explained that her job was to obey even if she didn't understand or agree with my reasons.

She still argued.

I finally said, "Take the shoes upstairs NOW. And when you're done with that job, I have another assignment for you. I want you to go into the living room and march around the coffee table seven times."

She stared at me, then began to laugh. "For a minute I thought you were serious."

I smiled back. "Actually, I'm very serious."

She did it. Shaking her head at her crazy mother, but she did it. Seven times. (As she was marching, my husband quipped, "Oh GREAT. Now all she has to do is blow a horn and the coffee table will collapse.")

We've had to repeat this exercise a few times since then (tonight I had her do ten jumping jacks in the den). But I think I'm getting my point across. Every time Kaitlyn argues with me or refuses to obey until I give her a reason she happens to like, I dole out a whimsical task that can't be argued with. I tell her to wash an imaginary elephant, or hop like a frog, or stand on her head in the corner.

I give her a task to which she can no longer ask, "But why?"

I give her a task that has one reason and one reason only: Because I said so.

Which makes me wonder about all the times I've argued with God.

I'm sure there are times he wearies of my backtalk. I'm thinking about the times he's asked me to do something—forgive someone or tithe consistently or quit gossiping or griping or doubting—and I've responded by saying, "But . . ."

"But WHY?"

"But you don't understand . . ."

"But NOW'S not a good time. Why can't I do it LATER?"

As far as I know, the Lord has never made me "practice" blind obedience by asking me to do something frivolous. (I've only been asked to wash an imaginary elephant once in my life, and it wasn't by God. I was thirteen and we were playing truth or dare, and it was either wash an elephant or admit that I'd let Robert Greilach kiss me in the fellowship hall after youth group.)

But I guess I'm saying that learning to trust and obey is something my heavenly Father desires for me as much as I desire it for my kids and my dog. Actually, even more so.

I'm teaching my kids to trust and obey. Maybe I should sign up for a refresher course myself.

I may not be a straight-A student, but I think I can do at least as well as the next guy.

Especially if the next guy wears a flea collar and answers to the name of "Walter."

31

Sometimes You Just Gotta Go

FRIENDS CONDALL AND KATHY CLEGG JUST BOUGHT A HOUSE an hour north of here. They've been members of our Sunday school class for a while now, so the class decided to give them a going-away present. We wanted to give them something for their new home. Something that would give them the chance, several times a day, to sit and think about the friends they left behind.

So we gave them a toilet seat.

Not just any run-of-the-mill toilet seat.

It was an AUTOGRAPHED toilet seat, signed by every member of our class.

You can imagine the possibilities.

Bernie and Anita wrote, "We are flushed with emotion at your leaving."

Steve and Karin wrote, "I hope this does not eliminate us as friends."

Larry and Nancy wrote, "To two real crack-ups. We will miss you, butt . . ."

David and Jeanette wrote, "We aimed to please. You aim, too . . ."

Despite the humor, it was a sad occasion. Their absence has created a real void. So to speak.

Not that good-byes aren't something I'm getting used to. Summer vacation is a logical time for families in transition to pack up and leave. And this summer, the Cleggs aren't the only folks within my close circle of friends to experience a movement. So to speak.

Larry and Nancy Rottmeyer are moving to Indiana.

Jerry and Cherie Spurlock are moving to Colorado Springs.

If you've read many of my books, there's a good chance you've read about some of these folks. Cherie and Nancy, for example, are founding members of the Cracker Barrel Friday Morning Breakfast Club. Together with Darla Talley and Linda Douglas, we've met together weekly for breakfast for several years now.

In other words, I don't think of any of these couples as acquaintances. I think of them as FAMILY, and here three of them are abandoning me within weeks of each other.

Which is starting to impact my checking account. Between going-away parties, dinners, and presents, it's costing me a small fortune. And I'm not even counting the cost of all the therapy I'm going to need when the last moving van pulls out of Dallas.

Actually, the account that's really getting overdrawn is located somewhere above my rib cage. I'm having to draw on emotional resources I didn't know I had as I watch these friends swap information on real estate agents, moving companies, and the proper way to assemble a wardrobe carton.

The good news is that we've never been so wired, as a society and as individuals, for communication. All these friends have home phones, cell phones, fax numbers, and e-mail addresses. Keeping in touch should be as easy as punching a "send" button or logging on-line.

I suppose if we wanted to, we could even get video software for our computers, which, if you ask me, is a lot safer than getting video technology for our phones. I don't know about you, but I don't always WANT to be seen while chatting on the phone. Just yesterday, for example, I negotiated a book contract with my editor while sitting in the only quiet spot in the house. It gave a whole new meaning to the phrase "taking care of business."

This summer, it's possible that someone you love is relocating, or perhaps you're the one doing the moving. I wish I had some good advice for you, but the only thing I can suggest is waterproof mascara.

How do we manage these kinds of losses in our lives?

I'm still figuring it out. But it helps to remember that, in the overall scheme of things, God's in control. I'm in his hands and so are my friends, and I have to think that—tucked securely in the same hands—we can't get too far apart, no matter how many miles stretch between us.

Transitions. Bittersweet. They signal endings, but new beginnings, too. And whatever our transitions might look like this summer—relocations, new homes or jobs, a teenager moving out, a five-year-old starting kindergarten, the marriage of a child, friend, or even a parent—it helps to take a deep breath and remember that "this too shall pass."

Besides, as stressful as change may be, it often gives birth to good things that could not have come about in any other fashion.

But in the meantime, I'm sort of sad. I need some consolation. Hey, I've got an idea! The Cleggs, at least, are still within driving distance. Maybe I should surprise them by visiting them in their new home. That would make me feel better.

Besides, I'm sort of curious about something, and a surprise visit would be a great way to find out. I'd love to know if, when it comes to enjoying our gift to them, the Cleggs are fairly regular . . .

. . . or if the best seat in the house is in the garage.

32

Freebie, Schmeebie

WE JUST SPENT FOUR DAYS IN LAS VEGAS. My husband attended a conference there, and I got to tag along.

Everybody asks, so I might as well 'fess up.

Yes, I gambled. The good news is that I only lost a dollar.

Wanna know my secret? The secret to losing just one dollar is to gamble—you guessed it—just one dollar. I walked up to a slot machine with twenty nickels, pumped them in, and lost every one of them, all in the space of less than a minute.

Which sort of begs the question, "And this is supposed to be fun beeecaaauuusssse? . . ."

It was hard to get away from the gambling. There were slot machines in the airport, slot machines in the gas stations, electronic billboards flashing Keno numbers in the restaurants. I asked my husband for a handful of quarters before I visited a public restroom just in case there were slot reels on the stall doors and I was required to line up three matching symbols before being allowed to go on inside.

Actually, the entire ground floor of our hotel consisted of a full-service casino, which was rather conspicuously positioned between the lobby and the room elevators.

One day I was walking past the casino, and I just had to stop and stare. There was so much commotion! Bells ringing. Lights flashing. Electronic games beeping and singing and clanging. Folks walking around clutching plastic token cups, roaming from game to game . . .

And I'm standing there, wondering why all this is looking vaguely familiar, when suddenly I think, "It's Chuck E. Cheese's for grown-ups!"

Really. The only thing missing was a sweaty employee in a mouse costume.

The other thing I found interesting about Las Vegas is the freebies. Hotels often give discounts on rooms and amenities, hoping you'll hang around and gamble while you're there. Complimentary meals are common. Our hotel, for example, offered a frequent-patron program that would have netted me free rooms, meals, and drinks.

With all that free stuff, I figure the only way they could get any more complimentary was if they also told me I was nice looking.

You know, I may not put much stock in gambling, but I have to admit that when it comes to the possibility of getting something for nothing, I'm as much of a sucker as the next guy. In fact, I joined a book club once because I could get five free books for a dollar. What I didn't realize was that I wasn't allowed to quit the club until I had purchased a number of books equivalent to the inventory of the Library of Congress.

I guess there's no such thing as a free lunch. Which is too bad, because most of us would love to get that lucky break, win the lottery, experience a windfall. We'd love to be the one to slide a nickel in the slot machine and get a thousand dollars in return (better yet, we nongamblers would love to have a FRIEND win the lottery or hit the jackpot and share their winnings with us!)

Unfortunately, life doesn't usually work out that way.

There's this school of thought, however, that says that life is filled with freebies. You've heard the cliché as often as I have. It says, "The best things in life are free."

But I have to wonder about that.

After all, the very best things in life—a strong and passionate marriage, intimate friendships, a vibrant relationship with our Creator—exact a heavy toll. They may be priceless, but they are not without cost.

They require hard work.

They require sacrifice.

They require an investment of heart and soul, time and effort, love and risk.

Indeed, the best things in life are anything but free. But maybe that's okay. Because the price we pay is just a token, really, in light of the priceless value we receive in return.

The Bible offers us a strange economy indeed. If we lose our lives, we'll find them. If we're last, we shall be first. If we give with a glad heart, it'll be given back to us pressed down, shaken together, and running over.

Over and over the Bible teaches us that, when it comes to following Jesus and loving people around us, yeah, there's a cost.

But it's nothing compared to what we receive in return.

Which, if you think about it, is a lot better odds than you'll find anywhere else. Especially in Las Vegas.

I should know. We got home from Las Vegas Wednesday afternoon, and I immediately headed out to the supermarket to buy a few things for dinner. When the cashier announced my total, I decided to pay with left-over cash from the trip.

I pulled out my wallet and began counting out bills.

I was a dollar short.

33

Takin' It to the Street

IT'S AUGUST, AND I'M ABOUT TO EMBARK ON AN ADVENTURE that is as American as motherhood, apple pie, and Nick-at-Nite. In fact, for many folks, this particular experience epitomizes the spirit of summer vacation like nothing else.

After all, what other experience gives you the opportunity to sweat, bicker, whine, battle boredom, and bond with loved ones all in the space of one week?

I'm talking, of course, about the family road trip.

The recipe for a road trip is simple. You begin with a handful of kids and one or two well-intentioned adults. Put them into a space the size of the average coat closet. Jostle, mix, and toss for five to ten days. Season with any combination of the following: PMS, road maps that appear to have been written by the Three Stooges, pent-up testosterone, fast-food wrappers, engine trouble, a half-eaten bag of pork rinds, "NO VACANCY" signs viewed through bloodshot eyes at midnight, surly teenagers, and preschoolers with bladders the size of peanuts.

When the car limps back to its driveway-of-origin, fling open the doors.

All that jostling and seasoning in close quarters will have fostered a certain fermenting/marinating kind of process. Sort of like Amish friendship bread.

Or composting.

In any case, what tumbles out of the car—in addition to sweaty, cranky family members—is something not quite as tangible (and definitely not as aromatic), but just as real nevertheless.

I'm talking, of course, about warm family memories.

Sure, some of that warmth gets generated from heated arguments, busted radiators, and the kind of emotional spontaneous combustion that can occur when normally civilized folks spend too much time confined together in close quarters.

But even memories of chaos and crises, in retrospect, can take on a certain charm of their own. In fact, in hindsight, some vacation foibles can become downright hilarious. After all, lots of folks believe that comedy is merely tragedy plus time, and they may be on to something.

Other warm family memories, however, come from genuine Kodak moments. Intimate connections that wouldn't have occurred back home in the rush of daily living. Sweet moments of bonding (and I'm not referring to the time the Tootsie Roll melts in the backseat and glues the two-year-old to the upholstery).

So that's the kind of thing I get to look forward to. Our trip begins in one week, which gives me a limited amount of time to compile all the little necessities we're going to need for our journey. On the list are car toys, snacks, an ice chest, Larry's Windham Hill CDs, my collection of Shania Twain tapes, sunglasses, road maps, and a prescription of Valium.

I thought about bringing Walter, but decided that spending five days confined in a car with a German shepherd was on par with a bad case of hemorrhoids: The experience wouldn't kill us, but we'd be so miserable we'd wish it had. So Walter will stay home. And we'll hit the road. And when it's all said and done, we'll spend twenty bucks getting film processed at Wal-Mart, two days unloading the car, and the next couple dozen years reliving the laughter and the memories.

Truth is, I'm looking forward to the trip. It's going to be an adventure. I know everything won't go as planned and that there will be surprises (some good, some not so good) along the way, but I figure if everything went EXACTLY as planned, I'd wake up to find I'd been dreaming, which would mean, among other things, that none of my pictures would turn out.

Unplanned chaos, ruts, and bumps. I sort of expect them when I'm on a road trip.

They're a little harder to accept in other parts of my life.

When it comes to my marriage, parenting, finances, career, health, and friendships, I'd just as soon go by the map, thankyouverymuch. No surprises. No detours, disasters, or delays.

Unfortunately, that's not how it works.

Which is one of the reasons I love Psalm 139. It's one of my favorite passages in the Bible. I love it because it's chock-full of comfort, whether I'm talking about an excursion on the road or a season of my life.

The whole Psalm, from top to bottom, is magnificent. Do me a favor and read it (or reread it) for yourself this week. But in the meantime, let me quote one of my favorite phrases, penned by King David to God:

"Where can I go from your Spirit? Where can I flee from your presence? . . . If I rise on the wings of the dawn, if I settle on the far side of the sea, even there your hand will guide me, your right hand will hold me fast" (vv. 7–10).

What a comforting thought for road-weary folk like me! And it only gets better. I love the part where David says to the

Lord, "You hem me in—behind and before; you have laid your hand upon me" (v. 5).

What a great image! Whenever I read this verse, I get this picture: I'm traveling down the road of life, and there's God. He's got me surrounded. He's in front of me. He's behind me. He's even above me, with his hand on my head. This is better than Mapsco, folks. Better than AAA. Even better than having a car with one of those fancy satellite links that slaps street directions on a computer screen on your dashboard.

Feeling a little road-weary? Had your share of bumps and detours? Feeling lost and in need of some directions?

Yeah, me too.

What a great time to remember that we belong to Someone who doesn't need a compass for directions. He doesn't look to the stars because he's the One who hung the moon. Best yet, if we let him, he's ready to lead us in the way everlasting.

Not even AAA comes close.

34

open Mouth, Insert Foot?

PEOPLE SAY THINGS TO ME ALL THE TIME that I'd just as soon not hear. One day a woman came up to me in a store. I'd never met her before in my life. She just approached me to pay me a compliment.

At least I think it was a compliment.

She said, "I just love your hair color! It looks so natural. What brand do you use?"

I guess it didn't look as natural as I'd hoped.

But I shouldn't feel too bad. My husband has had worse experiences. A college professor at the time, my husband had just finished teaching a class when a student approached him and, nodding at my husband's suit, said, "I used to have a jacket that exact same color. I made it into a pillow for my dog."

Sometimes the table is turned. Sometimes I'm the one who would love to make a comment or give a piece of advice, but I hesitate because I'm not sure how well my words would be received.

In fact, recently I was sitting in an airport when I thought of something I wanted to say to the woman sitting three seats away from me.

I wanted to say, "You don't have to yell. I don't know who you're talking to, but my guess is that whoever it is, they would be able to hear you even without the cell phone."

Of course, people who yell into their cell phones aren't the only folks I'd love to set straight.

There are other things I'd love to say—but never manage to get up the courage to do so. Here's the short list:

"I'd love to know the name of the store where you buy your clothes. That way I won't ever shop there by mistake."

"Your kids could be bottled and marketed as a form of birth control."

"You don't have to suffer with unsightly facial hair. Help is available. We have the technology."

"Booger alert."

I don't say these things because I'm afraid the person I'm saying them to will be upset or offended. Of course, if I REALLY wanted to get these sorts of things off my chest, I could always have them silkscreened on a T-shirt or bumper sticker. This is because people will communicate all sorts of things on their chests or bumpers that they would never say in real life. Remember the bumper sticker that said "Mother-in-law in trunk"?

Sometimes getting something off your chest isn't such a bad thing. Sometimes people are wise to take a chance and just spit it out. They're right to just walk up and say what's on their minds even though they're not certain how their words will be received.

Some of my best friends have done this with me. I remember the time my sister Michelle took a risk with me and said,

"You know, Karen, you seem angry all the time." Her words got me thinking . . . and into Christian counseling.

It took courage for her to speak up. She took a risk, and it paid off.

Maybe I should follow her example. Jump in. Take a risk now and then. Maybe not with total strangers talking too loudly into their cell phones but with folks I know and love.

Telling a friend who is angry or depressed, "I love you and I'm concerned about you," is one example.

I can think of another example of something I should be willing to say more often. Oh, I think about saying it a lot, but too often I hesitate to spit it out. I'm afraid my words might not be well received, so I just think about what I'd like to say, roll it around in my head now and then, never letting the marble drop down to my mouth and out my lips.

I'm talking about the phrase, "You need Jesus in your life."

I'm not saying I'm not willing to talk AROUND the topic. If I'm with a friend who doesn't know Jesus, I might talk about church or God or spirituality in sort of general terms. But when it comes to the bottom line, I'm chicken. I hesitate to get the words out of my mouth: "You need Jesus in your life. Not church. Not a belief in some nebulous big guy upstairs. Not angels or good karma or some book by the latest spiritual guru featured on Oprah . . . but Jesus."

Sure, there's a chance that my friend will scoff or disagree or get defensive.

But there's also the chance that she'll say, "I'm not sure what I need, but I know I need something. Maybe it's Jesus, after all. Tell me more . . ."

Some phrases are simply worth the risk. In fact, some phrases have such eternal significance that NOT blurting them out can have tragic results.

"You need Jesus" falls into that category.

"Booger alert" does not.

35

Chocolate Lovers, Unite!

I HAVE A WEAKNESS FOR CHOCOLATE.

And apparently I'm not alone! When my book came out entitled *Just Hand Over the Chocolate and No One Will Get Hurt,* I found out just how much women love chocolate.

I was signing books one day when a woman came through the line. As I was signing her book, she drew near, peered into my eyes, and said conspiratorially: "Never, never, NEVER eat chocolate with nuts in it."

I blinked. "Um, okay. Sure. Why not?"

She said with conviction, "The nuts take up valuable space."

The other reason I know how much women love chocolate is because of their e-mail addresses. I get e-mails all the time from readers, and more women than you might imagine have e-mail addresses such as "MsChocolate," "M&Mlady," and "Hersheyluvr."

Even the content of their e-mails speaks to their love affair with chocolate. I've received more than one note that says something along the lines of the following: "As soon as I saw your book I knew I had to buy it! I had no idea what the book was about. I had never read any of your other books. In fact, I had never even heard of you. But I bought your book because I love chocolate!"

So that's my new marketing approach. It doesn't matter what topic I'm writing on—sex, water heater repair, rules for chat room etiquette, new trends in facial hair removal technology for post-menopausal women—whatever the topic, I'm putting the word "chocolate" in the title.

Sure, it's incongruent, but who cares? After all, who would have predicted the success of the best-selling book *Zen and the Art of Motorcycle Maintenance* by Robert Pirsig?

Just think what he could have done if he'd used the word chocolate in the title.

Fact is, there's not much the world can dish out to us that a two-pound bag of M&M's can't solve.

One day scientists will confirm what women have known for years: Chocolate really IS one of the four major food groups.

So chocolate is a well-loved comfort food.

What other foods do I turn to when I'm stressed or blue?

I love to make microwave s'mores. I put a graham cracker on a napkin, sprinkle some chocolate chips on the cracker, then top with a large marshmallow. I microwave til the marshmallow puffs up twice its original size, then pull the whole thing out of the microwave and top it all with another graham cracker.

These are messy treats but worth the effort. I've nibbled them while watching TV. I've gobbled them while standing in front of the microwave, all stressed out with no one to choke. I've savored them with girlfriends at my kitchen table. I tried eating one while working at my computer once, but my fingers kept sticking to the keyboard. Other than that, they're a great all-around snack and comfort food.

Of course, the downside to comfort foods is that they increase my waistline and make my bathroom scale cranky. I know my scale's cranky when it keeps spitting larger and larger numbers at me.

I've seen talking scales in stores. Yeah, right. Like that's what I need first thing in the morning: some computerized voice announcing my weight for the world to hear. Don't scale manufacturers realize that there are some things better left unsaid? Besides, if I really wanted to know how much I weigh, I wouldn't go to the effort of weighing myself before I put in my contacts each morning.

Sometimes I wish I could find comfort in rituals with a lower calorie content. Maybe I could acquire a taste for comfort carrots. Or take up comfort jogging. Or develop the habit of comfort flossing.

Weigh-Down Workshop founder Gwen Shamblin has an interesting slant on comfort foods. She tells the story of feeling stressed and upset and craving an ice-cream sundae. This wasn't just any sundae—she was craving the mother of all sundaes, complete with bananas and chocolate and nuts and whipped cream and a few Pepperidge Farm cookies tossed in on the side for good measure.

But before she went to the kitchen, she went to Jesus. I don't remember the exact words of her prayer. But the content was powerful, and her message stuck with me. Paraphrased, here's what she prayed:

"Lord, you know I REALLY want that ice cream. And I'm going to head into the kitchen in a few minutes to get it. But first I wanted to come to you. Can you do better than that sundae, Lord? Can you comfort me better than all that sugar and calories and goop? Because if you can, here's your chance. I'm coming to you first."

She never made it to the kitchen. Instead, she was ushered into a precious time of praise and worship with her Lord, an experience that turned out to be far sweeter than Häagen Dazs and less fattening to boot!

You think it won't work for you? How can you be so sure? Look, if you're willing to give it a try, I will too. Next time we've got a death grip on the chocolate, let's take a breather and ask Jesus to comfort us instead.

Just take a few minutes to pray and see what happens. Maybe even read a chapter from the Bible and see if the Holy Spirit has something wonderful to say to us through those inspired words. After all, there's power in the Word of God, which certainly explains why the Bible is the best-selling book of all time.

Even if it doesn't have the word "chocolate" in the title.

36

Recycling Mom

A COUPLE DAYS AGO MY HUSBAND CAME HOME from work and went upstairs to change out of his suit. After changing, he joined me in the kitchen. We chatted for a few minutes before he said, "Oh, something interesting happened at work today."

I said, "Yeah?"

He said, "As usual, I was in and out of meetings all day. Met with the president a couple times. Staff meetings. Normal stuff. Had my jacket off most of the day, and kept noticing this splotch of red ink on my sleeve. I wondered if I'd dragged my arm through something on my desk. Couldn't figure it out."

I was getting a bad feeling about this.

He said, "It wasn't until everyone had gone home for the day that I was sitting at my desk and looked down and noticed something else."

I winced.

He said, "I noticed a big splotch of white on the front of my shirt. It was white on white, so I hadn't seen it earlier. Then I saw the blue streaks on the back of my sleeve, and the green flecks on my collar, and it dawned on me what had happened—I'd worn one of the girls' painting smocks to work."

Now, I'm not very dedicated about recycling. But every now and then I come up with an idea or two of which I'm pretty proud.

Recycling my husband's old dress shirts into painting smocks for the kids was one of them.

I just never figured they'd get recycled back into work-wear. Tie-dye, move over. The Linamens are starting a new trend.

Despite the painting-smock debacle, I probably should try to recycle more often. Plastic containers, cardboard, old newspapers, glass jugs—they're all acceptable candidates for the plastic recycling bin the city was kind enough to leave on my curb. I think the idea is that I'm supposed to put these things in the bin, the city hauls them away, and the next time I see them they'll be in the shape of sunglasses or cereal boxes or even a toilet paper tube.

I think I would use the recycling bin more if it were bigger. I mean, it's just the right size for milk jugs and applesauce jars. But it's way too small for the stuff I'd really like to put in there.

For example, my five-year-old is a tight squeeze, and the fourteen-year-old won't fit at all. And I could NEVER get my husband in the bin, at least not all in one piece.

Now, on most days I wouldn't dream of recycling my family. But there are always a few days each month when I'd be willing to trade them all in on a new kitchen appliance or two.

Funny thing though, it's always the same couple days each month. Luckily the feeling usually goes away before I can call Sears and negotiate a deal. It's probably a good thing the P in PMS doesn't stand for the word "Permanent." If it did, I'd have a new toaster oven by now.

On second thought, maybe the person who needs to spend time in the recycling bin is the woman who stares back at me from the bathroom mirror each morning.

Maybe the city could haul HER away and bring back someone nicer. More spiritual. Immune to PMS and mood swings. Better at housekeeping. (And as long as they're making improvements, a size 9 body wouldn't hurt!)

Do you ever look at yourself and think, "Wow. So many flaws, so little time!"

I do.

There are days I'd love to be recycled into something else.

In fact, if I could pick one thing for God to change about me—one thing for him to recycle into something better—the thing I'd ask for is a really nice helping of faith.

I'd love to be able to trust him more.

I'd love to stop second-guessing all the stuff he allows into my life.

I'd love to stop asking, "But why, Lord?" and start asking, "What?" and "How?" as in, "Okay, so what do you want me to learn from this?" or "How can you use this in my life and in the lives of folks around me?"

I think that's what I'd want. I mean, if I could be recycled and all.

But listen to me. I'm talking like getting "recycled" is a fictional concept, when really it's something the Lord does really, really well.

Why else would the Christian faith use words like "born again" to describe what happens when someone like you or me decides to follow Jesus?

Why else would the Bible call us "new creations," and say that, through our relationship with Jesus, "old things have passed away and all things become new"?

Truth is, the Bible brims with promises of new beginnings and second chances.

Over and over again, it tells the stories of folks like you and me getting to live new and improved lives because a relationship with Jesus is transforming us into something we could never be on our own.

And, to make it happen, all I need to do is say, "Okay, Lord, I'm all yours. Change me."

I'll admit these aren't always the easiest words to say (I wonder if plastic milk jugs want to be recycled into Saran Wrap, or if they complain a little now and then?).

But it's a prayer that God loves to hear, a prayer he's always ready to answer in a way that is best for me, after all.

Which, when you think about it, is a whole lot better than anything my city has to offer, and with no curbside waiting at that.

37

Don't Believe
Everything You Hear

I HEAR PHRASES ALL THE TIME that I have a hard time believing.

Take, for example, the phrase, "You're not getting older, you're getting better."

I know this isn't true. Much to my chagrin and dismay, I really AM getting older, and I'm reminded of it daily to boot.

You know you're getting older when you buy a rotary phone at a garage sale, and one of your daughter's friends tries to call home but can't because she's never seen a phone like yours before.

You know you're getting older when you walk into Supercuts, tell the hair stylist to give your kid a Dorothy Hamill, and she looks at you and says "Dorothy who?"

And you know you're really getting older when you take a road trip with your kids, and you need more potty breaks than they do. How come, as we age, the cartilage in our ears continues to grow while our bladders shrink?

One morning my friend Linda called me and said, "Did I wake you up?"

I told her, "Nah, my bladder did that twenty minutes ago. I don't even use an alarm clock anymore. If I need to get up earlier than usual I just drink an extra glass of water before bedtime and limit my nocturnal potty breaks to two."

Not to mention that weird thing that's happening to my memory. Take yesterday, for example. I looked at my five-year-old and said, "Kacie, go put the cheese away in the . . . the . . . that thing over there. You know. Right there. What's it called again? Oh yeah. The refrigerator."

All this might be fine and dandy if we lived in a culture where age and wisdom were revered. Unfortunately, we live in a society where youth and beauty are worshipped above all else.

Wealth and power are a close second.

I don't know about you, but it's easy for me to get sucked into the beliefs and values represented on TV, in literature, and in the lives of many around me. When I'm not careful, I find myself buying into the idea that more is better, that my personal comfort is the ultimate pursuit, that what I do is more important than who I am, that marriages are disposable, or that my value as a person is determined by my beauty, youthfulness, or bottom line.

When it comes to shaping my view of my world, my self, my purpose, my worth, and my relationships, I'm tempted to go to the world.

I could be going to the Word, instead.

God's perspective on my life, purpose, and worth should be the only one that matters. Yet I can spend merely minutes a day absorbing his perspective and hours each day soaking up the viewpoints of Tom Brokaw, not to mention those of Monica, Rachel, and Phoebe.

Another cliché I hear all the time is this: You can't teach an old dog new tricks. I don't know about canines, but I'm guessing forty-year-old women are as teachable as they want to be.

I think today I'll make an effort to turn off the world and turn to God's Word.

That is, as soon as I remember where I put my reading glasses.

Autumn

38

Help Is on the Way

NOT TOO LONG AGO I HAD "ONE OF THOSE DAYS."

I was feeling pressure from a writing deadline.

I had company arriving in a couple days, and the toilet was clogged.

I went to the bank, and the trainee teller processing my deposit had to start over three times.

I swung by the supermarket to pick up a few things, and the lines were serpentine.

By the time I got home, I was frazzled and sweaty and in a hurry to get something on the table for dinner. Deciding on Campbell's Cream of Mushroom soup, I grabbed a can opener, cranked open the can, then remembered I had forgotten to buy milk at the store.

Nix the soup idea.

Setting the can aside, I went to plan B, which was left-over baked beans. I grabbed a Tupperware from the fridge, popped the seal, took a look, and groaned. My husband isn't a picky eater, but even HE won't eat baked beans that look like caterpillars.

Really frustrated now, I decided on a menu that promised to be as foolproof as it is nutrition-free: hot dogs and potato chips. Retrieving a brand-new bag of chips from the cupboard, I grabbed the cellophane and gave a hearty pull.

The bag didn't open.

I tried again.

Nothing happened.

I took a breath, doubled my muscle, and gave the bag a hearty wrestle.

With a loud pop, the cellophane suddenly gave way, ripping wide from top to bottom. Chips flew sky-high. I was left holding the bag, and it was empty.

It was the final straw. I let out a bloodcurdling scream.

"I CAN'T TAKE IT ANYMORE!!!"

My husband heard my unorthodox cry for help. Within minutes he was standing at the doorway to the kitchen, where he surveyed the damage: an opened can of soup, melting groceries, moldy baked beans, and one quivering wife standing ankle deep in potato chips.

My husband did the most helpful thing he could think of at the moment. He took a flying leap, landing flat-footed in the pile of chips. And then he began to stomp and dance and twirl, grinding those chips into my linoleum in the process!

I stared.

I fumed.

Pretty soon I was working to stifle a smile.

Eventually I had to laugh.

And finally I decided to join him. I, too, took a leap onto the chips. And then I danced.

Now I'll be the first to admit that my husband's response wasn't the one I was looking for. But the truth is, it was exactly what I needed. I didn't need a cleanup crew as much as I needed an attitude adjustment, and the laughter from that rather funky moment provided just that.

So now I have a question for you, and it's simply this: Has God ever stomped on your chips?

I know that, in my life, there have been plenty of times when I've gotten myself into frustrating situations and I've cried out for help, all the while hoping God would show up with a celestial broom and clean up the mess I've made of things.

What often happens instead is that God dances on my chips, answering my prayer in a completely different manner than I had expected, but in the manner that is best for me.

Sometimes I can see right away that God's response was the best one after all.

Sometimes I have to wait weeks or months before I begin to understand how and why God answered a particular prayer the way he did.

There are even some situations that, years later, I'm still trying to understand. I figure God will fill me in sooner or later, either this side of heaven or beyond.

Do I trust him? Even when he's answering my prayers in a way that is completely different than my expectations—even when he's dancing and stomping instead of sweeping and mopping—can I embrace what he's offering? Can I let his joy adjust my attitude? Am I going to stand on the sidelines and sulk, or am I willing to learn the steps of the dance he's dancin' with my needs in mind?

I'll be honest with you: Sometimes I sulk. Sometimes I dance. I'm working on doing more of the latter than the former.

I guess the older I get the more I realize that he really does know what he's doing. He loves me and I can trust him.

Even when the chips are down.

39

Things I've Learned from My Kids

I'VE LEARNED LOTS OF THINGS SINCE BECOMING A PARENT.

For example, before becoming a mom I had no idea there was such a thing as "tinkle targets" you could drop in the toilet to give potty-training toddlers something to aim at.

And suction devices to suck snot out of newborns' noses? Well, I never saw that one coming in a million years.

And what about all those childproofing doohickies and doodads? Before becoming a parent, the LAST thing on my mind was rigging my toilet seat so that it would require seventeen minutes of labor, a master's degree, and an act of Congress before I could go to the bathroom.

Since becoming a mom, I've also learned about things like humility.

For example, several years ago I was at a booksellers convention having breakfast with two influential women I'd worked with for years. Linda Holland was a bigwig at my publishing company. Ramona Cramer Tucker was top dog at *Today's Christian Woman* magazine. And I was having the time of my life, because they were both sitting there bragging about my work. Linda was excited about my latest books, while Ramona had just asked me to become a contributing writer to the magazine and was excited about my articles. My head was swimming. If all the congratulatory back-patting I was giving myself was real instead of just in my head, my shoulder would have been pulled out of its socket by then.

About that time, Ramona turned to me and said, "But my favorite story about you—the one we tell around the office all the time—was from ten years ago. I had called you about some project, and we were talking on the phone, when all of a sudden you said, 'Hold on! I'll be right back . . . my toddler just stuck a peanut butter sandwich in the hard drive!'"

Just then Linda began to laugh. She said, "Oh, that's nothing. She has a new baby now, and last week I was on the phone with her when her daughter set the microwave on fire and gave the cordless phone a bath in the toilet."

I'm sure the whistling sound I heard then was just in my imagination. If anyone else had heard and asked about it, I would have said, "Oh, don't worry about it, that's just my ego deflating back down to normal." At least I hope no one else heard it. If they heard it and didn't ask, they might have assumed the windy noise was coming from a different source. Now THAT would have been REALLY embarrassing.

I've learned other things, too, from being a parent, sometimes during the most unexpected moments.

Like a couple years ago.

Kacie is five now. But when she was about two, she had this game she loved to play with her dad. It was sort of like hide-and-seek. Except she was never "it." She was always the one hiding.

What was really funny was that she always hid in the same two places. If we were upstairs, she covered herself up totally with the quilt on my bed. Every time. And if we were downstairs, she hid under the desk in my office.

Every time.

Sure, Larry would pretend this was a tough assignment. He would roam through the house saying things like, "I wonder if Kacie's in the refrigerator?" and then look in the refrigerator. Or "I wonder if Kacie's hiding behind the couch?" and then look there.

But ultimately, he knew exactly where to find her, because she always hid in the same place.

Which got me thinking.

You know, I do that.

When I'm hurting or confused or rebellious, sometimes I try to hide from God. But you know what? I always hide in the same places. I always run to the same old sins or distractions or addictions and try to hide behind them. I think I'm so clever, as if my heavenly Father doesn't know my tricks already. Like he doesn't know where to find me.

But the truth is that he knows where I am and, like the loving dad he is, he's willing to give me a little bit of time until I'm ready to be found. He lets me play my game until I get sort of cramped and lonely in that secret place of mine, and then he can't wait to scoop me into his loving arms.

If I made a list of the very best things I've discovered by having kids, this would definitely be on the list.

The nasal suction device would not.

40

Tandem Belching, Anyone?

AMAZING THINGS HAPPEN WHEN KIDS GET REALLY BORED.
We were driving from Colorado Springs to Dallas last week.
That means twelve hours in the car with no TV, telephone,
or e-mail. My kids went catatonic for awhile from shock and
grief, then they entertained themselves for awhile by bicker-
ing, and then they got creative.

I knew they had entered the creative stage when my five-
year-old said, "Look, Mom, I can burp!"

Kacie has always wanted to burp-on-demand just like her
fourteen-year-old sister, Kaitlyn. (I'm hoping as she matures
she'll get some new goals in life, but for now, I guess this one's
as good as any!) Intrigued, I turned around in my seat and
asked for a demonstration.

Kacie opened her mouth.

Kaitlyn, hiding behind a book, let one rip.

I started to laugh. "Interesting," I said. "Ventriliburping."

Suddenly I had an idea. There's something my five-year-old can do that her big sister can't. Kacie can whistle. Kaitlyn cannot. I told the girls my idea. They loved it!

In a few moments, Kaitlyn appeared to be whistling up a storm. It was Kacie, of course, providing the sound, but that didn't seem to stem the gleam in their eyes.

They were thrilled with their new skills. I was thrilled with something else they had discovered, whether they realized it or not.

I said, "See, girls? You need each other. Together, you can do things you weren't able to do on your own."

It's a lesson I hope they remember, because it'll come in handy time and time again.

The fact is, some things just go smoother when you have company. Zipping up that last two inches of a dinner dress falls into that category. So does shopping for a bathing suit. Holding a garage sale is something else that begs for collaboration with a friend.

And what about whining? Whining is definitely a two-party event. I've tried whining to my dog, Walter, but it's just not the same. He really doesn't know how to comfort me. The best he knows to do is get me a biscuit, which is what he wants when he whines, but it's just never worked for me.

So whining requires human partnership.

Laughing is the same way. Sure, it's possible to laugh alone, but the most healing hee-haws come in tandem. When I'm hurting, it feels good to laugh. This is because, when life gets tough, we have two choices: We can cry about it, or we can laugh, and laughing is easier on the mascara. Crying makes me look like a raccoon.

So I laugh when I can. And when I can't, I go ahead and embrace the masked mammal motif and have myself a four-hankie bawl. Crying is one of those activities that can go either way: Sometimes I cry by myself. Other times it's healing to cry with someone who loves me.

Depression is another experience that begs for help from others. Oh sure, I'll admit that my first reaction when I feel overwhelmed, stressed, or depressed is to isolate myself. Withdraw. Disengage. But I've done it enough times now to know that it doesn't help. In fact, it only makes things worse. For one thing, there's no one around to listen to me whine. For another thing, those doggie biscuits are starting to taste like sawdust.

The Bible recognizes our need for human companionship. Best yet, it gives lots of examples of intimate relationships. Some were based on romance. For example, God made Eve because it wasn't good for Adam to be alone. Solomon wrote passionately about his lover. Even the animals got to bring dates on a romantic forty-day cruise.

And yet intimate companionship isn't found in romantic relationships alone. Naomi had Ruth. David loved Jonathan. The disciples traveled in pairs, reaping encouragement and strength from hanging with others who loved the Lord.

I used to think all my needs for intimacy and companionship were supposed to be met by a husband. Now I know that God brings all sorts of people into my life to help me do and be what I could never accomplish or become on my own. This is because there are so very many things I just can't do on my own.

Luckily for everyone involved, burping isn't one of them.

41

Holiday Traditions
Worth Remembering

MY HUSBAND TELLS THE STORY of the time his mom made rice pudding. No one could figure out why the pudding had seeds until Mom realized she was supposed to have cooked the rice.

Then there was the time Larry's grandmother made a pumpkin pie, which was an impressive endeavor considering that advancing years had relieved her of most of her eyesight. Two days later, she had the chance to serve a slice to her son and daughter-in-law. Jan took one bite and said, "Mom, you left the wax paper on the pie crust." Grandma said, "That explains a lot. That was the toughest crust I've ever eaten."

And she should know. She'd already gnawed her way through half the pie.

The thing that makes holiday recipes so special is the fact that we only make them once or twice a year.

That's also what makes them so scary.

I have a hard time remembering things I do every day, like picking up my kids from school or taking my Prozac. Remembering how to do something I only attempt once or twice a year is out of the question. Every time I have to renew my car registration, defrost a turkey, or dust off a beloved holiday recipe, I feel like I'm having to feel my way through the process for the very first time.

This is why my favorite holiday recipe goes like this: "Go to the freezer section. Open the door. Select the box with the best-looking photograph. Return home and slide the frozen pie into your own pie dish. Bake. Serve. Hide the box."

Homemade rice pudding with seeds? My family should be so lucky. The last time I made homemade rice pudding, I was dishing it up when my spoon hit something bigger than a seed but smaller than a breadbox.

At least I'd found the pot holder.

What I'm saying is that, at least for me, executing once-a-year recipes is a challenge. The other challenge I face is trying to find the festive items I only need during the holidays. This year, my list of AWOL holiday props includes turkey-shaped Jell-O molds, the box of Christmas decorations, and the animated reindeer head that sings, "I'm dreaming of a white Christmas, just like the ones I used to know . . ."

Sometimes I think there should be a dry run. Maybe in August or September. Then we could practice all our Thanksgiving recipes and hire Magnum P.I. to locate all the Christmas decorations. That way we'd be practiced up when the real holidays came around.

In fact, maybe we could send practice Christmas cards during summer vacation, just to make sure our mailing list was up to date. And we could serve July 4th barbecue on our very best china just so our dishes wouldn't feel too unfamiliar come Thanksgiving. And that cornucopia centerpiece? Wouldn't it look great holding Easter eggs or a nest of chocolate bunnies?

And when it comes to holiday attitudes like gratitude or worship, what would happen if we dusted those off as well and used them during the other ten months of the year? What if, at the end of this month, gratitude didn't get packed away with the pilgrim-shaped salt shakers or the pinecone turkeys your kids crafted at school? What if worship of God and good-will toward men didn't get stored in the attic with the nativity set and the reindeer lawn art?

The bottom line is that some things are just meant to be enjoyed year 'round.

My husband says pudding with seeds probably isn't one of them.

42

How to Survive Cold and Flu Season

I HAB A CODE.

I took some cold medicine, but it's taking a while to kick in, and until it does I'm sounding a little like Elmer Fudd on Xanax.

Of course, even then, my medicine will only help my symptoms. It won't really cure me. This is because they say there's no cure for the common cold.

My friend Beth discovered this the hard way. For the past year, Beth has been saving pennies for a cruise. A big deal, this cruise—everyone in her family was going, including grandparents, cousins, and kids. Two weeks before she was supposed to sail into the best vacation of her life, Beth showed up on my doorstep waving two bags from the pharmacy down the street.

Seems she had visited her family doctor and obtained prescriptions for every ailment known to womankind. She had pills for bladder infections. Patches for motion sickness. Birth control pills to postpone her period. These were mostly preventative measures. Beth wanted to board the boat prepared for every conceivable malady. She was adamant that nothing—no virus, bug, or menses—would interfere with this vacation of a lifetime.

Two days before her trip, Beth came down with the grandmother of all colds. Her postnasal drip was so bad, she didn't need an antihistamine, she needed a plumber. If you didn't get any presents delivered to your house this Christmas, it's because Rudolph took one look at Beth's nose and filed for unemployment.

Nothing in Beth's bag of pharmaceutical tricks could help. Rest and time proved the only remedy. Beth went on her cruise anyway. It didn't help that when the ship sailed into some fog, the captain said the horn was on the blink and asked Beth to blow her nose instead.

This was a month ago. Now Beth is sick with something else. I think the doctor said whooping cough. The funny thing is that Beth's a nurse. I told her she needs to quit bringing her work home with her.

I also showed up at her home with a little something to make her feel better.

If I were Martha Stewart, it would have been homemade chicken noodle soup or a casserole. But I'm not, and so the thing I brought was a half-gallon tub of ice cream. Cold hands, warm sentiments. Beth understood.

Colds are equal opportunity ailments. They don't discriminate. Everybody falls prey, even the folks who are supposed to take care of the rest of us when we get sick. I know it's disconcerting when it happens—I mean, I get a little worried when the doctors and nurses around me are sicker than I am—but there's only one thing to do when it happens.

Don't gawk or point a finger. Instead, pitch in with some caregiving of your own.

The truth is, whether we're talking germ warfare, emotional valleys, or spiritual struggles, folks who minister aren't immune. Sometimes they fall under attack. Sometimes they need an encouraging word, some wise instruction, a healing touch, and time to recoup just like the rest of us.

Know someone under attack? Someone you thought was invincible? Don't gawk. Instead, pray. Send an encouraging card or e-mail. Make a phone call. Lend an ear. Provide a shoulder. Offer a hand. Provide a Kleenex. Give a hug. Bake a casserole. Babysit her kids. Show up with a gift that shows you understand and that you care.

A carton of Rocky Road and two spoons is a nice place to start.

43

creepy crawlers

HARALD CALLED ME YESTERDAY WITH A STORY that will send any arachniphobics among my readership into therapy.

Harald is my brother-in-law. He and my sister Renee live in Oak Harbor, Washington, with their three boys, six goldfish, and a tarantula.

The tarantula is a new addition. One week ago, their family roster did not include a spider the size of carry-on luggage.

It all started when my sister Renee decided to go away for the weekend. She was going to a women's retreat. As she was heading out the door, her husband announced that he would be taking the boys to the pet store because seven-year-old Hunter wanted to buy a pet. Harald added, "He wants a tarantula."

"Absolutely no tarantulas," Renee said. "If a spider like that ever got loose in the house, I'd have to move into a hotel. No Best Western, either. I'm talking Hilton."

The next day Harald and the boys were driving in the van, Hunter cradling a glass terrarium on his lap, when Harald said, "Oh yeah. Don't let it get loose in the house or Mom'll have to move to a motel or something."

They arrived home and carried their furry friend into the house. Less than an hour later, one of the boys was holding the terrarium when it fell to the floor and broke into tiny pieces. Harald spied the eight-legged wonder sitting dazed among the glass. He rushed to pick it up. The spider promptly bit Harald's finger. Harald flung the spider to the ground, where it scurried under a kitchen cabinet.

Harald looked at the clock.

Renee was due home in two hours.

Armed with a flashlight and broomstick, Harald probed the small hole into which the black spider had fled. No luck.

Returning from the garage, Harald plugged in a 6.5 horsepower ShopVac capable of suctioning the dimples off Joe Namath. But it couldn't lodge an arachnid from a cabinet.

Undaunted, Harald headed back to the garage. When he returned a few minutes later, he was brandishing an electric saw.

By now several neighborhood husbands had learned of the crisis and gathered 'round to offer hearty masculine support as piece by piece, Harald began sawing apart his cabinets. The cabinet floor beneath the sink went first. Then various toe-plates. Then bottoms of drawers.

They finally found the tarantula in the last possible section of cabinet.

The furry interloper was safely imprisoned in a borrowed terrarium when Renee walked in the front door.

She immediately said, "What happened here?"

Harald said, "Why do you ask?"

"There's a 75-pound Shop Vac sitting on the white carpet in the middle of the living room, that's why. What's going on?"

The men in my sister's life—all four of them, from the midlifer down to the preschooler—looked her in the eye and said, "Nothing. Nothing happened. Everything's fine."

Around the corner in the kitchen, the cabinets lay in pieces, and sawdust was still settling around the flashlights, saws, and ShopVac attachments.

I imagine Renee was about to figure it out on her own. She didn't have to. Hunter confessed. Then, to make up for all the commotion his pet had caused, he decided to do something extra special for his mom.

He named the spider in her honor. He named it "Mama."

We can learn a lot from this story. We can learn to avoid women's retreats, staying home instead to protect our homestead from well-meaning husbands and venomous spiders larger than most of our body parts.

Renee says that, besides the women's retreat thing, the experience is also teaching her to face her fears. She says, "I don't want to steal Hunter's joy over this pet. So I'm working on putting aside my fears. I make a conscious effort to go look at the tarantula at least once an hour, sometimes twice, just to desensitize myself. Not to mention to make sure he's still in his cage."

Sort of like living with Hannibal Lecter.

Life's like that, isn't it? Sometimes our worst fears come home to roost. Sometimes someone leaves, or someone dies, or the stock market crashes, or the doctor clears his throat ominously before delivering the news, and we think, like Job in the Old Testament, "Here it is. This is it. The thing I have feared has come upon me."

And then we get on with the business of coping, which includes, but isn't limited to, activities like crying and whining, which eventually, if we're lucky, begin to morph into other things, things like accepting and trusting and growing.

I wish you and I could be protected from everything that goes bump in the night. Instead, we have a God who says,

"Yes, they'll go bump, but let me hold the flashlight, and we'll face it together."

And who knows? When it's all said and done, maybe we'll come out ahead, in possession of things we couldn't have gotten any other way, things like mettle and strength and spirit. Not to mention an eight-inch-long spider named "Mama."

44

Clean Sweep

I **WENT THROUGH THE CAR WASH THE OTHER DAY.**

Of course, that wasn't my intention.

My intention was to send MY CAR through the car wash. It's just that things don't always work out like I'd planned.

I had just picked up my daughters and a couple of their friends from school when I decided my car needed gas and a wash. I filled up the tank of my 4-Runner, paid for the gas and a car wash, and received a receipt with a code printed in red ink.

I drove up to the car wash tunnel, punched in my code on a little keypad, got a green light, and drove forward.

My front tires hit a bump. The light flashed RED. I was supposed to stop right there, right on that bump, and let the brushless magic begin. I sat. I waited, but the sprayers sat silent. I realized I had overshot the bump that triggers the sprayers.

I popped the transmission into reverse, backed up an inch or two until I was exactly on the bump. Still nothing. I backed all the way out of the tunnel, back to the keypad, unrolled my window, and punched in my code again. The green light beckoned me forward, letting me know that all was forgiven and that my car wash could commence.

Darned if I didn't overshoot the bump again.

I started to back up to the keypad again, but now there was a car waiting behind me. I was trapped.

I opened my car door and ran back to the keypad and punched in the code.

So now I'm standing at the keypad, and my car is sitting in the car wash tunnel, the driver's door wide open and the front tires planted firmly on that malicious little bump, which is apparently exactly how the car wash imps wanted everything arranged, because at that moment the sprayers kicked into action and began dousing everything—me, my car, my driver's side upholstery—with a generous layer of pink suds.

I ran through the sudsy maelstrom and jumped into the front seat, slamming the door behind me. My hair was matted to my head with pink suds. I wiped my forehead clear of pink foam dribbling toward my eyes. The four girls in the car were laughing so hard I thought they'd need CPR. The woman sitting in the BMW behind me had a pinched look on her face, as though she were wondering if I might be dangerous as well as stupid.

But at least my bumpers were spic and span. Come to think of it, my car didn't look half bad either.

There's something about a clean car. I love it. Know what else I love? A clean house. I love it when the beds are made and the countertops are clean and the clutter is contained (let's add fresh-baked bread in the oven and homegrown veggies in the sink and maybe even Ricky Martin sitting at my kitchen table. Why not? We've obviously crossed the line into La-La Land).

The problem with getting a clean house is that I hate cleaning. Well, not ALL houses, just my house. Other people's houses are another story. I mean, is it just me, or have you noticed that it's a lot more fun cleaning someone else's house rather than your own?

I like puttering around in my friends' kitchens. After a meal, I don't mind at all whipping up some soapy water and starting with dishes, gravitating to pans, and wiping down all the countertops and appliances when I'm done.

And clutter? While my own clutter stumps me daily, I'd know just what to do with that pile of sewing supplies sitting in one friend's living room or the stack of newspapers, mail, and last month's schoolwork sitting in the kitchen of another.

Sometimes I even look at other messes in my friends' lives, messes they've made or wandered into, and find myself thinking, "Why, that's not such a mess at all. That'd be easy to clean up. I know EXACTLY how she should go about tidying that unruly marriage, or that child's difficult attitude, or all those broken dreams and secrets she's been sweeping under the rug for years."

Of course, MY messes continue to stump me, just like the clutter in my house. Sometimes, in fact, I get so used to MY messes and clutter that I wonder if I'm seeing them clearly or if my vision is being impaired by something in my eye, something sort of, well, kind of like, you know . . .

A log.

You probably know that Bible verse as well as I do, the one that says "How can you see to clear the speck out of your sister's eye when you've got a log hanging out of your own?"

The truth is, making a clean sweep of things isn't always as easy as it seems, whether the tidying up needs to occur in my life or yours. Which is why I, for one, am going to stop applying the White Glove Test to the homes and lives of my friends. Instead, I'm going to love them best I can and try in the meantime to stay open to any housecleaning the Holy Spirit wants to do in my own life.

In fact, I wouldn't complain at all if he started with my hair.

I had no idea those pink suds would be this hard to get out.

45

crazy for cocoa Puffs

LAST WEEK A FRIEND OF MINE SAID, "You should meet Susan. She's really disciplined about what she eats. She's so disciplined she even puts padlocks on her fridge and pantry so she doesn't eat anything fattening."

I hate to burst anyone's bubble here, but Susan is NOT disciplined. A better word to describe Susan would be "creatively impaired." This is because any woman in the throes of a binge—any woman with an ounce of imagination, that is—would not be deterred for a heartbeat by the presence of a mere padlock on the freezer door. Nosiree.

A lock means nothing. It's kind of like wearing a T-shirt onto the floor of an Amway convention that says, "No. Please. Stop. Whatever you do, DON'T tell me how I can achieve financial freedom AND be my own boss without ever leaving the comfort of my living room."

I figure, when it comes to the mood to binge, where there's a will there's a way. For example, if MY fridge were padlocked, I'd head for my kids' stash of Halloween candy. If all the good candy happened to be gone, I'd reach for my car keys. And if for some reason I wasn't able to find the keys to my car, no problem.

Ever see a woman rumbling into a Dairy Queen on a riding mower?

Sometimes a woman's gotta do what a woman's gotta do.

Padlock on the fridge? C'mon. Give me a REAL hurdle. Something with teeth.

I have other addictions, too. Junk food isn't the only one. The other thing I'm addicted to is mail order catalogs. I get so many catalogs that two years ago my mailman canceled his gym membership, and his forearms still look like Popeye's. There's so much processed pulp around my house that my address is listed in the National Directory of Forests and Forestry.

But that's all. Just junk food and junk mail. Everything else in my life has some sort of redemptive value. Well, okay, almost everything, except for all those mindless TV shows I love. But that's it, I promise. Just junk food, junk mail, and junk TV.

Which is okay, right? I mean, it's just entertainment, right? So my figure is about as curvaceous as a Twinkie. I'm starting to believe I deserve all those catalog offerings I covet, and I've practiced for so long that I can watch TV for hours now without even the slightest twinge of conscience.

But it's all in fun.

Right?

Of course, when it comes to bingeing on junk food, it's easy to know when I've overdone it. My scale, body shape, energy level, and even my blue jeans don't hesitate to scold me when I get too far out of line!

But what about those other binges? What about when I've binged on head candy—when I've filled my brain with ideas or images that are materialistic or hedonistic, when I've lusted after lifestyles or laughed at plot lines promoting values I don't embrace. What happens then?

It's so easy to get desensitized.

Several years ago, my friend Cherie Spurlock taped an index card above her TV. On it were these words, taken from Philippians 4:8: "Whatsoever things are true, whatsoever things are honest, whatsoever things are just, whatsoever things are pure, whatsoever things are lovely, whatsoever things are of good report; if there be any virtue, and if there be any praise, think on these things" (KJV).

If I took that verse to heart, I'd definitely want to cut back on the head candy, those nutrition-free binges of input that fatten up my sin nature and leave my spirit clogged and lethargic.

Maybe this wouldn't be a bad subject to bring up with family and friends. Maybe we could encourage each other to think about what we put into our brains. Maybe we could talk about making healthier choices. Maybe we could even figure out how to take that verse from Philippians and make it come alive in our own daily walks.

I think these would be great conversations to have.

I think they'd be even greater if we had them over root beer floats. Meet me at Dairy Queen. I'll be the one on the John Deere.

46

Spin Doctors

So the other day I'm sitting there watching the surgery channel.

No, really. I'm serious. I don't know if they actually call it the surgery channel, but that's what they do. They show operations. Real surgeries on real patients. It's actually very cool.

So, anyway, I'm watching the surgery channel when my husband walks up behind me and stands there watching the screen for several minutes. Finally, his eyes still transfixed on the TV, he says, "So what is this, a cooking show or something?"

I say, "No. They're replacing a kneecap."

Larry never answered. He just made this strange gurgling noise as he careened from the room.

I don't know why I like the surgery channel. Maybe for the same reasons I like psychology, dieting (when it works!), and snorkeling: Because sometimes it's fun seeing what's hidden under the surface.

Of course, I'll be the first to admit that some things that are undercover should stay that way. My own personal kneecaps fall into that category. We've been close for years, my kneecaps and I, but I've never actually laid eyes on them, and I'd just as soon our relationship stay that way.

But for the most part, I love figuring out what makes things tick.

This is probably why my girlfriends and I can dissect a problem for hours and never run out of angles to discuss. We should all get jobs on national TV, like those men and women who can fill literally hundreds of hours of airtime analyzing an eleven-minute presidential speech.

Except I don't want to analyze politics. I want to analyze things that really matter, like kids and husbands and frustrations and dreams and goals. How to cope is good for at least a two-hour conversation on any given day, as are weight loss and various beautification procedures. You'd be amazed how much mileage my girlfriends and I can get out of talking about unwanted body hair alone.

Sometimes, the outcome of all this analyzing and dissecting is that we stumble onto some very workable solutions. Other times, the best we can do is table our conversation until the next time we're together, when we pick up pretty much where we left off. Not unlike a miniseries. Except this one goes on forever, kind of like *Shogun* seemed to do except with far more commercial interruptions, most of which look uncannily like children.

But I have a question. What if we CAN'T figure it out? What if we dissect, analyze, probe, brainstorm, and whine ad nauseam and we STILL can't get it solved? "It" could be anything, anything at all. "It" might be a clueless husband, a demanding career, a rebellious kid, stubborn love handles, tenacious creditors, or a long, dark spiritual tunnel in which we're not entirely sure whether the light ahead is the light of day or an oncoming train.

I have a couple problems like this. Problems I've been dissecting for years. Which is fine, because I think it's good to study and ponder and even whine now and then as we try to figure out the enigmas of this thing called life.

But I'm starting to wonder if there's not a time when it's right to put down my tweezers and my microscope, when it's best to fling wide my hands and say, "Okay, Lord, all my intellectual prowess hasn't gotten me diddly as far as this problem is concerned. So I'm taking a break, here. Please remove this problem from my life YOUR way, or show me why it's here, or help me trust you, or something. But I'm going to stop tussling with it like a puppy with a dishtowel. I'm going to stop working so hard. It's yours. It's in your hands. I'm taking a vacation."

In time, maybe we'll go back to wrestling with our problem, because, after all, God gave us these brains of ours for good reason. But whether we do or don't, taking a break and putting a long-term problem squarely in the capable hands of a loving heavenly Father might be just the ticket.

Besides, think about how good it would feel to relax a little. And if we're whining less, imagine all the spare time we'd have. In fact, now that my problem's in good hands, I think I'll kick back and watch a little TV.

I hear there's a tonsillectomy on at three.

47

Quack, Quack

LAST NIGHT BETH AND I WENT OUT FOR COFFEE. She's in the middle of remodeling her bathroom and was feeling stressed with her husband and kids and the plumber and the tile man and just pretty much life in general.

So we ended up in a booth at Chile's.

We scanned the menu, ordered two cups of coffee, the tuna fillet and grilled veggies, then went back to discussing Beth's stress and the fact that she was down to her last nerve.

Little did we know that our waiter was about to find that last nerve and walk all over it.

It started when he brought coffee, sugar, and cream but no silverware.

Beth spent the next five minutes trying to wave him down. After she asked for silverware, he brought forks but no spoons.

Another five minutes passed as Beth tried to get his attention. When she did, she growled, in a voice reminiscent of

Linda Blair's in *The Exorcist,* "We'd like some SPOONS here." He apologized and promptly brought us two long-handled iced tea spoons that would have made it possible for us to stir the coffees of the couple sitting four booths away.

By now I was trying hard not to laugh, and Beth was trying hard not to make headlines in the next morning's paper: "Waiter in Critical Condition after Being Bludgeoned by Spoon-Wielding Midlife Mom."

I looked across the table at my friend. "I have three little words that will save you."

She asked, "What are they?"

I said, "Be a duck."

She said, "Excuse me?"

I said, "A duck. Be one. Okay, close your eyes. Take a deep breath. Visualize with me. You're a duck. The clueless waiter is a drop of water. He falls on your feathers. He rolls right off. Water off a duck's back and all that. You're not even wet. Let it go, Beth. Let it roll right off. Take a deep breath and let it go. Be a duck. Say 'I'm a duck.'"

She closed her eyes and said, "I'm a duck."

(See why I love my friends?)

I said, "That's right. Be a duck. Be a duck. Be a duck."

She opened her eyes and flashed me a wicked grin. "You know, this is going to come back to haunt you the next time you're upset about something."

I laughed. "I know. And when my turn comes, don't worry. I'll be a duck, too."

I love figuring out new ways to cope with the stresses and messes of life. When life hurts, what helps? Indeed, my last two books have been dedicated to answering that very question—each book contains more than a dozen tried-and-true ways to feel better when life throws you a curve.

Although I have to admit, the duck speech came out of the blue. It was a new one even for me. But I think it helped, and I'm definitely going to try it myself the next time I feel my blood start to boil.

I wish you and I were immune to crisis, but unfortunately we're not. Emotional crises, family crises, health crises, beauty crises, even trainee waiter crises—we're subject to them all, aren't we?

Not long ago, however, I experienced a crisis even I wasn't prepared for. It was a crisis of faith. I'm writing about this because last week I got a letter from a woman named Deborah who wrote, "I've been living on antidepressants for the past year and am struggling with my faith."

And I could really relate, because a couple years ago I found myself in a lot of emotional pain, and somehow, in the process, my faith took a real beating as well.

Now, I've met folks and I'm sure you have, too, who—when crisis comes a callin'—say, "My faith is the thing that got me through."

One of my girlfriends was like this. Jenny was diagnosed with breast cancer at 32, brain cancer at 35, and was a citizen of heaven by 37. But in the meantime, everyone who loved her got to watch her faith grow into something massive and muscled and strong, an Arnold Schwarzenegger–sized faith, and it was a beautiful thing to see.

In MY times of crisis, however, my faith becomes an eighty-pound weakling that couldn't get me out of a soggy paper sack.

Not all the time. But more often that I like to admit.

I'm happy to say, however, that the thing that gets me through—even when my faith is knock-kneed and anemic and in need of an awful lot of handholding and antibiotics and maybe even CPR—isn't a thing at all but a Person.

A couple years ago I was in such emotional pain that I was having a hard time walking with the Lord. To be honest, I wasn't even trying. And when it came to prayer, the best I could muster was a single plea, and for months these were my only words to God, and they went like this:

"Lord, hang on to me. I know I should be hanging on to you, but I'm not. The truth is, I feel too wounded and broken and angry and rebellious and hurt right now to hang on to you. So if I'm going to get through this at all, it's got to be up to you. See me through this, Lord, hang on, please hang on to me and don't let go."

And guess what?

He hung on.

When life hurts, what helps? The list is long: laughing, crying, counseling, working out, music, insightful sermons, caring friends, gardening, whining, praying, reading, reflecting, and even quacking come to mind.

But sometimes everything seems to fail, even our faith. In other words, sometimes we quack and sometimes we crack.

Even then there's hope. Because even when our faith's not strong our God is faithful.

Daisy, Daffy, and Donald don't know what they're missing.

48

Lose the Loose Ends

If only split ends and loose ends had more in common.

When it comes to split ends, all I have to do is change shampoos, get a haircut, or wear a hat.

Loose ends are another story.

My life seems filled with loose ends. I'm talking about projects I've started or things I need to take care of that just keep hanging around. And around. And around. Not even the Energizer Bunny is as persistent as some of the loose ends in my life.

My house is filled with unfinished projects. There are chairs to be painted and clothes to be donated and articles to be written. Last spring I bought draperies for the living room. They've been sitting in a bag on the floor in the corner for months.

And then there's that thing I do with photo frames. I buy them. I display them around my home. The thing I never seem to get around to doing is filling them with photos of real-life people I know and love.

In fact, if you come to my house, glance at a sofa table, and see a framed photo of an attractive person with cover-girl looks on par with Christie Brinkley's, then turn to me and say, "Who's this?" there's a chance that I will answer, "Oh, that's my mom" or "that's my daughter." There's also a good chance I'll shrug my shoulders and confess I have absolutely no earthly idea. That's because you'll be looking at a photo of some anonymous model hired by the company that sells the frames.

So you can see that I have lots of good intentions.

Sometimes I run a little short on results.

Which I guess is okay, except for the fact that all this "unfinished business" can make me feel overwhelmed. In fact, sometimes my loose ends get so numerous that I can't go five minutes without stumbling over one of them and feeling, well, sort of undone by all the details that keep slipping through the cracks.

I guess I could try to get more organized. That would be one approach. I've tried before, of course, and it hasn't worked, but I'm willing to try one more time. (FYI: If I ever DO succeed and become a paragon of organization, you'd better get right with God because this is definitely a Sign And Wonder, perhaps even of the Last Days variety, which means there may be merely hours, even minutes, before Jesus returns.)

I guess the other thing I could do while I'm thinking about getting organized is relax a little. Loose ends aren't the end of the world, right? I mean, BIG loose ends like forgetting my kids and leaving them standing in the carpool line over spring break is something to be avoided, but maybe LITTLE loose ends like the fact that visitors think I'm related to Christie Brinkley aren't the shameful failures I tend to think they are.

That's the real problem right there, isn't it? That feeling of failure. You see, when I have unfinished projects hanging around, I start to wonder if I'm a big fat failure. I think of the sterling work ethic on which our Great Country was founded, and I start to hear fifes and drums and a patriotic voice-over that sounds uncannily like George C. Scott saying, "Would Betsy Ross have unfinished draperies lying on HER living-room floor for six months? Would Caroline Ingalls be four months late on a writing deadline? Would Martha Washington have photos of toothy blonde models sitting on her coffee table? Of course not!"

But on better days—when I remember to ask the Lord to quiet the yammering jaws of George and any other accusing voices in my head—I'm able to think of my unfinished projects in a brand-new light.

After all, I'm not the only one around here with an unfinished project. There's someone else I know who specializes in Works-In-Progress, which is just another way of saying Not-Done-Yet, and HE'S not a failure. In fact, he's Lord of Lords and King of Kings, and the biggest unfinished project he's got going on at the moment that I happen to be aware of is, well, me.

So there it is, the simple truth that brings me comfort and hope. It's like Paul wrote to the Philippians: "For I am confident of this very thing, that He who began a good work in you will perfect it until the day of Christ Jesus" (1:6 NASB).

So the next time I see something I'm still working on, I'm not going to feel bad. I'm going to take it as a reminder that I'm not so different from that unstitched cloth, that I'm a work-in-progress, that I'm in good hands.

I'm also going to stop beating myself up about the things I've yet to finish. I take after my Father, after all, and you know we creative types just can't be rushed.

49

Boy crazy

KAITLYN IS ON THE PHONE WITH A BOY.

His name is John and he's been calling every day now for a couple months, and they would both be MORTIFIED if they knew I was writing about them this very minute.

I'm not sure I'm ready for this. Anybody out there got any suggestions?

How did this happen? I mean, it wasn't all that long ago my sister and I were sprinkling glitter on the windowsill trying to convince Kaitlyn that's where the tooth fairy got into the house.

A couple years before that, Kaitlyn was starting every morning by crawling out of her crib, padding to my bed, patting me awake with her hand, and saying, in a very measured and articulate manner for a two-year-old, "I want SOMEthing to eat and SOMEthing to drink and carTOONS on TV."

Before that she used to sit in her diaper in the front of the supermarket cart and gnaw on animal crackers and frozen broccoli (yes, I said frozen broccoli) while I did my shopping for the week.

And now she's fourteen and she borrows my shoes and she's on the phone with a BOY.

Actually, there's a part of me that thinks this is going to be fun. Despite the moments of panic I'm experiencing on a nearly daily basis, I'm sort of enjoying the process and promise of ushering her into young womanhood.

A couple months ago, for instance, I took her and one of her friends, Amanda, to the opera.

The week before the performance, we went shopping, and the girls bought strapless formal dresses at an outlet store. Driving home in the car, they made plans. Kaitlyn said, "Let's do each other's makeup for the opera."

Amanda said, "My sister-in-law said she'll come over and fix our hair!"

Kaitlyn said, "I'm going to get my nails done."

Amanda said, "I think I'll wax my brows."

Kaitlyn sighed. "Too bad there won't be any guys our age at the opera."

But I was glad.

I was glad that, for this first foray into grown-up dress-up, there were no boys involved. I was glad the girls were enjoying their feminine beauty not to impress some testosterone-drunk teenaged boy, but just, well, just because.

I couldn't resist the opportunity. I said, "You don't need boys at the opera. Do you think a boy would notice that you waxed your brows? Of course not. It takes a GIRLfriend to take one look at you and say, 'Ohmigosh, you waxed your brows! They look GREAT!' Dress up for your girlfriends. Dress up for yourself. Dress up for the fun of it. But don't dress up for boys. They won't know how to truly appreciate the effort!"

The girls laughed, the sort of two-faced laugh that appears to say on the surface, "Yes, Mother-dear," but in reality is being used to communicate to each other the sentiment, "Just humor her. She doesn't know anything about boys. She's old."

But the truth is, I know how easy it is for women to get caught up in a hunt for approval and affirmation from men in their lives. I know how easy it is for us to define our identities and derive our value based on (a) whether or not we have a boyfriend or husband and (b) what we think these male-gendered folk think of us.

Unfortunately, this tends to be a fairly reliable recipe for disappointment and disaster. This is because men don't REALIZE they are functioning as the genesis of our self-esteem. They think their role is mostly to bring home a paycheck and occasionally, maybe around Valentine's Day, buy us a new garage door remote. If they only knew that their every word and deed (or lack of word and deed) is the hammer and chisel by which the very identities and self-worth of their women are being shaped, they would probably, instead of being such an overall clueless class of individuals, decide to stay bachelors much longer.

Of course, the Bible tells me that there is one Man in whom I can safely place my identity, one Man whose love for me makes me valuable, one Man whose thoughts about me are more numerous than the grains of the sand and the stars in the heavens.

I want to communicate this to Kaitlyn before it's too late. With God's help, maybe I have a chance.

And in the meantime, I'm going to go on enjoying the process of teaching her the finer points of being a woman.

I'd better go now. She just finished waxing her brows, and I want to be the first to notice.

50

Good Gifts

THE OTHER DAY I CALLED MY FRIEND LINDA AT HOME.
When she answered the phone, she sounded groggy.

I said, "Sorry, did I wake you?"

She said, "No, you didn't wake me."

I said, "Oh, well, for a minute there it sounded like I woke
you up."

She said, "You didn't."

"That's good." I changed the subject. "So what're you doing?"

She said, "Actually, I was taking a nap."

I was still chuckling at that one when Kaitlyn came home
from school. She was grumbling because she'd been late to
school that morning and now she had detention.

I said, "What did you expect? Fifteen minutes after you
were supposed to have walked out the front door, you were

still standing in your pajamas in the bathroom. Of course you were late to school. You should have been ready sooner."

She said, "But Mom, I *was* ready. The only thing I had to do was put on my clothes."

I call this the Barry defense, after Washington mayor Marion Barry, who once said of his fine city: "Outside of the killings, we have one of the lowest crime rates."

So I'm sitting here feeling like I've been missing out on a growing trend, the trend of optional logic.

I think this is a helpful trend.

The only trend I can think of that would be even more helpful would be the trend of optional calories.

Then we could say things to waiters in restaurants like, "I'll take a double slice of the caramel turtle cheesecake in the edible white chocolate bowl for ten calories."

I think ten calories is a reasonable amount to have to spend for a rich, gooey dessert that's larger than a full-grown trout, don't you?

This makes much better sense to me than the current system, which is to assign an ironclad number of calories to tasty foodstuffs, especially since the number that gets assigned is always a very large number, so large, in fact, that scientists sometimes borrow it to count the number of galaxies in the universe when it's not, of course, being used to identify the calories in, say, a single chocolate kiss.

So optional calories would work for me.

So would optional stress.

Speaking of stress, friends George and Nancy invited us to spend a weekend with them at an oceanfront beach house in Galveston.

I hate it when that happens.

Don't get me wrong, I like the beach. And I love these friends. But sometimes packing, planning, and getting out the door for a two-day vacation can seem daunting, especially when you're already feeling overwhelmed.

So that's where I was two days ago, feeling stressed and overwhelmed and like the last thing I could handle at the moment was getting everybody packed up and out the door.

Luckily, Beth dropped by right about then and literally pushed me up the stairs. "Go pack," she said. "I'll finish your dishes and round up the kids and make sandwiches for the road, but you WILL be out the door in half an hour or else you'll answer to ME."

Sensing that staying home could be hazardous to my health, I packed.

And I'm glad I did. As I'm writing this, I'm looking out a bank of open windows at my kids playing in the waves not twenty yards away. Beyond that, there are dolphins dancing in the swells. There's an ocean breeze cooling the house, and the sound of the waves breaking is a never-ending lullaby. It's a familiar sound. Sometimes, in the springtime, the wind rushing through the trees around my house sounds just like this, just like the ocean. Sometimes I close my eyes and imagine that I'm at the beach. It's one of Nature's more soothing voices, and I've heard it in the wind, and I'm listening to it now, in the waves just a stone's throw away.

And to think I might have been at home obsessing about the stress in my life.

What was I thinking!

The Bible tells me that "every good and perfect gift is from the Lord." I believe it. But, unlike things like stress and calories, these good gifts really are optional—I can choose to push them away, or I can embrace them with open arms.

I wonder how many good gifts I've left unopened because I was too stressed, harried, or just plain shortsighted to recognize them for what they were?

My life feels crazy sometimes. I know that yours does, too. There are lots of things we'd just as soon do without in our lives, but we don't always get to choose what goes and what stays. Which is all the more reason to embrace the good stuff God sends.

I'd say "stop and smell the roses," but that's so cliché.

Instead, walk on the beach. Putter in your garden. Bicycle down a road made emerald by a canopy of treetops. Watch your kids play. Spend time with good friends. Listen to the wind. Take a deep breath, a nice break, a long nap. And while you're doing it, think good thoughts about the God who sends moments of respite into lives reeling with busyness.

And don't forget to laugh. Laugh whenever you can, as loud as you can. Laughter is healing. It's contagious. Best of all, it's free. And if there's nothing humorous in your life at the moment and you need a good chuckle, call Linda. She should be taking a nap right about now.

Karen Linamen is the author or coauthor of nine books and is a contributing writer for *Today's Christian Woman* magazine. Formerly an editor with Focus on the Family, Karen is a frequent speaker at church and community women's events. She lives with her family in Duncanville, Texas.

Karen also loves hearing from readers and can be reached at the following addresses:

thefunnyfarm@email.com

Karen Linamen
P.O. Box 2673
Duncanville, TX 75138